George Washington's
New Jersey

Independence was declared in Philadelphia.

It was won in...

George Washington's
New Jersey

A Guide to the Crossroads of the
American Revolution

Including a Narrative of
New Jersey's Key
Role in the Fight for Liberty

Craig Mitchell

Middle Atlantic Press
Moorestown, New Jersey

Cover Design: Vicki Manucci and Terence Doherty
Interior Design: Vicki Manucci

For information write:
The Middle Atlantic Press
10 Twosome Drive
Moorestown, NJ 08057

When news spread through the family that this book had been accepted by a publisher and would see the light of day after many years of work, most of the family said "Congratulations" or "Wonderful news" or something similar. Granddaughter Amanda (11), six feet in the air over her trampoline, immediately shouted, "Who are you going to dedicate it to?"

So after considerable thought, this book is dedicated to Amanda, her sister Megan, and her cousins Alex and Joanna. They have been lucky. Their mothers and their grandmother have been overexposed to Revolutionary War sites for too many years, have perched on too many cannons, have stumbled across too many overgrown fields, have peered through too many dusty windows. For all of which, I thank them.

CONTENTS

PHOTOS

Preface

Forget Saratoga. Forget Yorktown. George Washington really fought and won the Revolutionary War in New Jersey. Here he fought not only the British army, its Hessian mercenaries, and its local Tory supporters, he also fought smallpox, mutinies, traitors, lack of food, clothing, arms, gunpowder and, especially, money. He also battled with the Continental Congress, with state legislatures, and even with some of his own subordinate generals.

Between 1776 and 1781, the most trying years of the Revolutionary War, George Washington spent more time in New Jersey than anywhere else. He fought more battles in New Jersey than anywhere else. Martha spent more time with him here than anywhere else. He suffered more setbacks, and gained more victories here than anywhere else. More places connected with the wartime Washingtons are open to the public, visible and visitable, in New Jersey today than anywhere else. This is a guide to those places.

There are both military battlefields and headquarters where organizational and supply battles were fought. There are private homes that were opened up and made available to Washington and his lieutenants. These are true "colonial" homes – built, that is, when New Jersey was a colony. They provide information and insights about life in the eighteenth-century that is available in no other way.

Many of these places have been rescued and preserved by local citizens interested in saving these remnants of America's history. State and federal funds have been used in many cases, but in quite a few the effort has been entirely by private organizations and local people. Many of these homes today are staffed and preserved entirely by local volunteer efforts. This book is in thanks to these volunteers.

Introduction

George Washington and New Jersey

Depending on how you look at it, New Jersey has the fortunate or unfortunate position of lying between New York City and Philadelphia. Ben Franklin called it "a barrel tapped at both its ends." Also, for good or ill, New Jersey, peninsula-like, is surrounded by an ocean and two major navigable rivers. Of its 480 miles of border, only 48 are land miles.

During the Revolutionary War, New York City was the major base of the British army while Philadelphia was the capital of the rebelling colonies. This strip of land in between was a major area of tension for most of the eight years of war. It's been called "The Cockpit of the Revolution."

In 1775, the nation as a whole was still divided as to whether it wished to part from Great Britain. Roughly one-third strongly wanted to be independent and another one-third — their brothers, sisters, fathers, mothers, cousins, sons, daughters — strongly wanted to remain under the King. This produced a classic civil war of relatives and friends bitter with each other. The remaining one-third weren't sure what they wanted and would sway with whatever winds happened to prevail for the next vicious years. In New Jersey, for many, it was also the continuation of a religious war that had been going on for several decades between the Old Lights and the New Lights of the Presbyterian Church and the similar *conferentie* and *coetus* of the Dutch Reformed Church. This religious aspect made the family quarrel even nastier.

Before the war, New Jersey was noted as one of the most beautiful, plentiful areas in the nation. Already it was being called "The Garden" of the colonies. Every traveler who came through New Jersey wrote home about its beauties and commented on its lush growth, bountiful harvests and attractive vistas.

George Washington, when the war started in 1775, was a 43-year old plantation owner and local Virginia politician. As a fatherless young man of 14, he had been sent into the wilderness of western Virginia as a surveyor's helper, and at 18 had entered active duty in the west with the Virginia military forces. At 22, he was made commander in chief of the Virginia troops. In a minor skirmish with the French in the wilds of Pennsylvania, his men fired the shots that started the French and Indian War.

He was a major factor in guiding and assisting British General Braddock in his march to combat the French at Fort Duquesne. He led Braddock's army in its retreat after its disastrous battle with the Indians. Washington resigned his post at age 26, in disgust that as a full colonel he was outranked by the greenest ensign in the British army, solely because he was a colonial. Some historians say that this animosity propelled him throughout the Revolution.

During the tense period of disagreements with Britain that led up to the outbreak of war, Washington, a member of the House of Burgesses in Virginia, was also elected to the Continental Congress. Here, when the cold war became hot in April 1775, and the Congress began casting about to find a commanding general for the army in front of Boston, Washington showed up in his Congressional seat wearing his Virginia colonel's uniform. He was quickly elected as the commander in chief.

At Boston, he learned the size of his problems. First, and most serious, the almost total lack of gunpowder, then, short enlistments, troop commanders elected for their popularity rather than their experience or ability, and a lack of common training. Also, there was a shortage of all kinds of supplies, a lack of money, artillery, and cavalry.

He solved the gunpowder problem in a way that would become typical of his actions throughout the war. While casting around among the various state governments, frantically trying to scrounge up a supply, he arranged to lose a letter to the Congress right where the British could find it. In the letter, he complained to Congress that he badly needed more storage buildings for his huge supply of gunpowder. The British conveniently found — and believed — the letter and refrained from attacking. (This from the man who "could not tell a lie.")

He found a fat Boston bookstore owner, Henry Knox, who had a textbook knowledge of artillery, and sent him to Ticonderoga in the middle of the winter to bring back the train of artillery from that fort. Knox succeeded and became one of Washington's most trusted advisers for the rest of the war. Washington mounted the guns on Dorchester Heights overlooking Boston on the southeast, and forced the British to depart that city on March 17, 1776.

The British army quickly shifted its headquarters to New York City in the summer of 1776 and remained there until November 1783. By the middle of August 1776, there were 35,000 British and Hessian troops based on Staten Island, the largest British expeditionary force ever sent overseas until World War II.

In the years ahead, Washington learned many things about being a general that a backwoods Virginia colonel would never have faced. He would never have enough money or supplies, but he would get longer enlistments and would build a truly continental army officered by men chosen for their ability not their popularity or their position in the community. He would put down mutinies, overcome palace politics, and — against the advice of leading doctors of the day — would inoculate his troops against smallpox. He would pen the major British force within New York City and eventually bring them near to starvation. He would have his men well-trained by an obscure Prussian baron named von Steuben. And in the end, he would win the war.

New Jersey, the "Garden" colony, would become the most battered of the thirteen original states. It would see more major battles than any other state. It would see more — and nastier — raids and counterraids by its citizens than any other state. Whole villages would be burned out, even their churches destroyed. Its loyalists would seek revenge by raiding patriot farms; patriots would in turn take vengeance against their neighbors and former friends who supported the king. The state's once-bountiful harvests were reduced by the scarcity of farmers to create them. And what harvests were reaped were carted away by one or the other hungry army. Their homes were stripped, their farms bared, their wives and daughters ravished. By the end of the war, the whole of northeastern New Jersey was devastated. It had, indeed, been the cockpit of the war.

Today, New Jersey has many remnants of the War of the Revolution — forts, battlefields, barracks, campgrounds, and houses which Washington and his generals used as headquarters. Even the smallest villages in northern New Jersey have their own stories and markers or monuments of Washington's presence. They represent an irreplaceable historic treasure. Enjoy them. Learn from them. Be inspired by them.

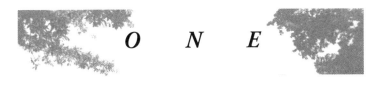

O   N   E

The Long Retreat Begins

In the autumn of 1776, Washington had been trounced by the British at Brooklyn, been pushed out of Manhattan, forced into Westchester, and had fought a drawn battle at White Plains. His only strong point east of the Hudson River was a fortification at the northern end of Manhattan proudly called Fort Washington. This fort and its twin across the river, Fort Lee, were designed to keep British warships from sailing up the Hudson River. They were unsuccessful.

Fort Lee was named for General Charles Lee, one of the odder characters of the Revolution. He was a former officer in the British army who migrated to America just a couple of years before the war started. Congress was very happy to have him in its service and named him second-in-command to Washington. He considered himself to be a military genius, one much better equipped than his superior to run the army and direct the war. He was tall, almost ludicrously skinny and was always accompanied by his pet hounds. After the Battle of White Plains, Washington had left a large body of troops with Lee to remain in the Hudson Valley at North Castle and protect the river from British invasion. We'll hear much more of him later.

On November 14, 1776, Washington and his chief assistant, General Nathaniel Greene, inspected Fort Washington. Greene insisted that it could be held. Washington was doubtful but didn't want to second-guess one of his most trusted generals. Washington finally agreed to its defense.

Two days later, Washington and Greene watched from Fort Lee as British and Hessian troops under General William Howe demolished the defenses and captured the fort with little trouble, capturing or killing 2900 of Washington's limited forces and, almost equally important, capturing tons of ammunition, supplies, and cannon.

This loss was a turning point in George Washington as a commander. He wrote to his brother Augustine, "[Fort Washington] was held contrary to my wishes and opinions." From that point on, Washington would listen courteously to the opinions of others but in the end would follow his own "wishes and opinions." He was growing in his job.

Four days later, the British took Fort Lee with no fight at all. British General Lord Charles Cornwallis had created an almost unbelievable maneuver on a cold rainy night in late November. He crossed the Hudson River from Spuyten Duyvil, at the northern tip of Manhattan Island, with 4,000 men in whaleboats, then Cornwallis and his men climbed the precipitous New Jersey Palisades in the dark of night on a narrow little path that sloped up at about a 45-degree angle, dragging their cannon after them. As one British officer wrote home: "Our disembarkation appeared terrible and impracticable as we landed at the foot of a rocky height and had to go up a very steep and narrow path. Fifty men would have sufficed to hold back the entire corps if they had only hurled stones down on us."

The garrison at Fort Lee was warned in mid-morning by a local countryman on a plow horse. Frantically, the frightened militia-men scrambled out of the fort, leaving behind all their huge mound of supplies, including 9,000 tents, their artillery and their ammunition.

Fort Lee is actually on a peninsula, between the Hudson and Hackensack Rivers. The only crossing of the Hackensack was at the small hamlet of New Bridge, about five miles away. The men of the garrison ran for the road down the backside of the Palisades (today's Fort Lee Road), through the English Neighborhood (today's Leonia and Englewood) with its futile Liberty Pole. They cut through the woods on today's Liberty Road into Schraalenburgh (now Bergenfield) and down the road to the New Bridge (now in New Milford and River Edge), littering the road behind them with discarded gear.

Cornwallis's men entered the fort without trouble in the afternoon. Fortunately for Washington's army, they rested there. After all, they had already completed a hard and triumphant day's work. The general let them rest for a few hours, then sent an advance guard down the hill, along the easily-followed trail of the hastily retreating army. If he had been able to move more prompt-ly and had gotten between the retreating army and the New Bridge, Washington's army would have dissolved on the spot. But Cornwallis's maps were not accurate and showed New Bridge much farther south than it actually is.

It was pouring rain on a cold November evening as the panicky retreating army slogged through the mud from Fort Lee to the New Bridge. As they came across the bridge, they saw General Washington standing on the porch of the old Jersey Dutch stone home of Jan Zabriskie on the west bank of the Hackensack River. Earlier, they had seen Washington at the Liberty Pole, directing traffic and trying to bring order out of chaos. As the last of the soldiers straggled past, Washington boarded his horse and set out slowly for the village of Hackensack, about four miles south. That night, Washington wrote to General Lee, still in the Hudson Valley, "This country is almost a dead flat, and we have not an entrenching tool, and not above 3,000 men, and they very much broken and dispirited, not only with our ill success, but the loss of their tents and baggage. I have resolved to avoid any attack though, by so doing, I must leave a very fine country open to their ravages." It was a long, sad day.

Washington told Lee to cross the Hudson and bring his 9,000 men down to join him. He wrote to General Heath, with whom he had left 4,000 troops near West Point, and to General Schuyler, at Ticonderoga on Lake Champlain, to send as many troops as they could safely spare. And finally, he sent messages to the local militia leaders telling them to come to his aid. Schuyler agreed to send about 1,300 men under General Gates. Heath said he would send 600. Lee sent a list of reasons why he couldn't send anybody and also why half of Heath's force should be sent to join *him*. None of the militia responded at all as New Jerseyans watched and waited to see who would emerge victorious.

That night, the British advance guard camped on the east bank of the river. Barely more than a musket shot away, on the west bank, Washington's troops lay in the mud with no shelter since all of their tents were still back in Fort Lee. The next day the whole army followed Washington as he continued his retreat through Hackensack, Ackquackanonck (now Passaic), and into Newark, where he tarried until the British caught up with him. Then on past Elizabeth to New Brunswick, where he tried a short artillery duel with the British across the Raritan River. Then retreating again to Princeton and Trenton until, finally, he crossed the Delaware River, safe from further chase because every boat for miles around had been moved to the west side of the river at his direction.

New Bridge, the village of Hackensack to the south, and the sprawling hamlet of Schaalenburgh to the north went through about six weeks of terrible shifting sands that foreshadowed the bad years to come. On November 23 the British captured New Bridge and Hackensack. Local Tories, many in the green uniforms of British Volunteers, came out of the woodwork. The next day, with a mob of local Tories, they proceeded north up Schraalenburgh (pronounced Skrawlenburg) Road, spreading targeted destruction as they went. The home of the patriot pastor of the Schraalenberg church, Domine Dirck Romeyn, was a special target in what is now Bergenfield. His home was trashed and set on fire as were the homes of several of his prominent lay people. The plundering went on almost up to Tappan, just over the border in New York State.

When Washington left Westchester County after the Battle of White Plains, he left about 6,000 troops with General William Heath at West Point. When Washington began calling for help in New Jersey, Heath moved many of these troops south and aligned them along the New Jersey-New York border line, from the Hudson River to the Ramapo Mountains.

Two weeks after their first raid, the Tories marched north again, aiming for Tappan. This time they ran into some of Heath's men and were turned back. Five days later Colonel William Malcolm and a body of Heath's men took their own raid south to The Flatts (present Oradell and New Milford), about three miles north of the New Bridge. This put the local Tories into panic. But five days later General Heath with 600 men pushed all the way to Hackensack. So New Bridge changed hands for the third time in less than a month.

After Cornwallis chased Washington across the Delaware into Pennsylvania, he did the usual European military routine: he sent his army into winter quarters. The 26th Regiment of British Regulars was sent to Hackensack, and the 7th Regiment went on to New Bridge, where they settled in for the winter.

Two weeks later, after Washington had picked off the garrisons of Trenton and Princeton, it was obvious that none of the small British winter posts was safe from him. On January 5, the 7th and the 26th regiments packed up their tents and went back into New York City. The bridge changed hands for the fifth time in less than two months.

For the next four years, the New Bridge would be the center of a "neutral ground," or "no man's land" between a British outpost at Paulus Hook (now Jersey City) and the advanced American outpost at Paramus church, four miles to the north. It was fought over constantly, either by organized forces or by little bands of Tory or patriot partisans. Recently, when the old shingle roof of the Steuben House was repaired, it was found to be riddled with musket bullets.

Bergen County, New Jersey, was probably the "most Dutch" area of all the original colonies. It was also a primary focus in a bitter internal brawl in the Dutch Reformed church. This was a decades-long battle between the evangelical "New Lights" or *coetus* side of the church and the conservative "Old Light" or *conferentie* side. This argument split families apart and created divisions that were still in existence early in the twentieth century. The battle resulted in the creation of a Dutch Reformed seminary in the United States for the first time, thus was Queens College (later Rutgers) begun.

When the Revolution began, the New Light families, almost unanimously, fought on the patriot side, and the Old Lights became Tories. Of the 44 ministers of the Dutch church, only three were Tories. Thus, in the area around New Bridge, the Revolutionary War was, in fact, a religious civil war — father against son, brother against brother. This made it extremely bitter and intensely fought.

The Zabriskie brothers were an example of this. Jan, Jr. who owned his father's mills, house, and business at New Bridge would forfeit them and move into New York as a loyalist. His brother Peter, at whose home in Hackensack Washington stayed, became an ardent patriot.

Fort Lee

Fort Lee Historic Park
Hudson Terrace (201) 461-1776
Open Wednesday - Sunday, 10-4:30. From Memorial Day to Labor Day, there is a $4.00 parking fee per car. No fee the rest of the year. Take first exit off the George Washington Bridge from New York, or the "Last exit in New Jersey" from Routes 4, 46, or 80. Go east to Hudson Terrace, south to the entrance on left.

Today, a replica of a typical fort of the time has been built near the site of the original Fort Lee under the auspices of the Palisades Interstate Park Authority. From your vantage point, about 400 feet above the river, the views of the Hudson, Manhattan, and the George Washington Bridge are magnificent. In the distance on a clear day you can see the Statue of Liberty.

There's a fine little museum in the Visitor Center where a short film is shown telling the story of the original fort. Views from the roof are magnificent, looking down at the Hudson River and across at the northern end of Manhattan. The walk along the top of the Palisades leads to reconstructed artillery positions, a typical stone hut to shelter the soldiers, and other military structures of the times. A large pavilion overlooking the George Washington Bridge is available for picnicking. The park is operated by the Palisades Interstate Park Commission.

Inland from the cliffs was a large army encampment with a square bastioned fort in the middle of it. The business district of the town of Fort Lee now covers it completely. Another part of the fort was built at the foot of the cliff where Burdett's Ferry was based. This is now covered by the Borough of Edgewater, and nothing is visible of the original installation.

Alpine
Blackledge-Kearney House
"Cornwallis Headquarters"
Palisades Interstate Park (201) 768-1360 or (201) 461-1776
Open Saturday and Sunday, 12-5, in April and May, September and October. Go north on Hudson Terrace from Fort Lee Historic Park to a T-crossing and go right, down the steep side of the Palisades to Englewood Boat Basin at river level. There are excellent picnic facilities here, too. About three-quarters of the way down the hill, the road forks off to the left (north). Take this along the foot of the Palisades about five miles following signs to Alpine Boat Basin.

This area was known as Closter Landing during the Revolution because the village of Closter was at the top of the narrow path used by local farmers. The Blackledge-Kearney House was a tavern frequented by local rivermen who lived and worked in this area at the foot of the steep Palisades.

Though there's no written proof of it, local folklore holds that British General Lord Charles Cornwallis stayed here, out of the rain, while his troops scaled the precipitous cliffs. Then he himself climbed the slippery path.

You can follow the path of Washington's retreating army by

going west on Fort Lee Road (the main street of the town of Fort Lee), down to Grand Avenue. Go right on Grand into Englewood, then left on Palisades Avenue, Englewood's main business street. Go to the traffic circle where the Liberty Pole stood during the Revolution, then right on Liberty Road. Pass the National Guard Armory on your left and go right at the light on Washington Avenue. The first left is New Bridge Road. Follow this across the new bridge to the first stop light then left and left into the parking lot.

River Edge
Historic New Bridge Landing
1200 Main Street (201) 487-1739
This is a textbook example of public/private cooperation in historic preservation. In 1995 the New Jersey State legislature created the Historic New Bridge Landing Park Commission to plan and carry out the development of a premier historic village based on several structures already in existence at the site. Cooperating are Bergen County, and the three municipalities of New Milford, Teaneck, River Edge, the state's Division of Parks and Forestry, the Bergen County Historical Society, and the Blauvelt-Demarest Foundation. Federal money has also been promised.

Three eighteenth-century houses, a nineteenth-century barn, a pivoting nineteenth-century swing bridge, and a modern replica of an eighteenth-century cook house are already on the premises. Nearby land has been purchased for a large parking lot and two buildings on the east side of the Hackensack River (one pre-Revolutionary) have been acquired, and other purchases are being negotiated.

When completed (in about 2008) it will be a major park facility comparable to Sturbridge Village in Massachusetts or Williamsburg in Virginia. Present facilities include:

Steuben House
Open year-round, Wednesday - Saturday 10-12 and 1-5. Sunday 2-5. Free. Take State Route 4 to Hackensack Avenue, Hackensack (by Riverside Square Mall). Go north, keeping to the right past the stores and bear right at signs for left turn jug handle. Turn right at the foot of the ramp when the first old stone house is visible.
The oldest part of this house may date to as early as about 1695. It was added to in 1714 and again probably about 1752.

Washington had his headquarters here several times, most notably when he sent off from New Bridge his brilliant young cavalry commander Colonel Henry "Light Horse Harry" Lee for a raid on Paulus Hook (Jersey City). Despite a confusion of difficulties, the raid was a spectacular success.

Jan Zabriskie, the pre-war owner, was a miller and merchant. A 90-foot dock along the Hackensack River accommodated ocean-going sailing ships. His mill, operated by tidal power, had two runs of grindstones. Iron products from the hills and farm products from the flat lands were shipped out from Zabriskie's dock to pay for the British finished products that came in here. A general store made this the commercial center of the area.

But Zabriskie was a Tory, and the house and grounds were confiscated by the government. When the war was over, the state presented the property to Baron Von Steuben in thanks for his contribution to the United States during the war. Steuben kept it for a few years but then sold it to move to Utica, New York. It was bought by Jan Zabriskie's son.

Today the Steuben House is owned by the state of New Jersey and is maintained as a State Historical site. Inside, it is furnished entirely from the collection of the Bergen County Historical Society. All the furnishings are authentic eighteenth-century pieces and are from the Bergen County area. The state owns one acre of ground on which the house sits. The Society owns the surrounding 17 acres.

If Washington were to return today and revisit all those sites where he is known to have slept or been headquartered, New Bridge would most likely be one of only a few he would recognize. Zabriskie's big old house with its long sheltering porch still sits by the river. There is still a bridge in the same place. Although not the same bridge, it is ancient enough to give the idea. Across the bridge, beside an 1890's boat house on the river bank, stands an old building that was a tavern in Washington's time. Visible through the crumbling blacktop are the old cobble stones that paved the road in front of the tavern, where the horse-drawn "Flying Machine" completed its run from Paulus Hook.

Tall trees line both banks of the river, as they did then, and the inexorable tide rises and falls. It wouldn't be hard to recognize.

The Demarest House

This house was built in neighboring New Milford, probably in the early 1770's. It is a typical example of a young Jersey

Dutchman's "starter house." It consists of two rooms with separate entrances. The right hand room was the parent's bedroom. The left hand room was the family room – living room, dining room, kitchen, rec room and all. Upstairs is an open loft for storage and where the children slept. Beneath was a basement for cold storage of vegetables. During the Revolution the owner was a member of the local militia.

The Campbell-Christie House

This house was also moved here from New Milford to save it from being bulldozed. It represents the next step up for the Jersey Dutch family. It is four rooms with a loft and a basement and a typical Dutch gambrel roof. It is thought to have been a tavern in Revolutionary times and is being furnished as such. The tavern-keeper is thought to have also been a militia member.

Both of these homes are open on second Sunday afternoons during the year. An 1850's English-style barn, and an outdoor kitchen made of antique stones but built recently, complete the property.

The bridge across the Hackensack is an iron-truss swing bridge built in 1888. It pivoted in the middle and was turned by a hand-crank. Young boys from a nearby school used to hop on the bridge and ride it around as it turned, their legs dangling over the sides.

A small brook runs along behind the buildings on the east bank. This brook is possibly the oldest still-existing political boundary on the continent. It was originally the boundary between the Hackensacki Indians to the south, and the Tappan Indians to the north. The Tappans sold their land beside it to David Demarest in 1677, and the Hackensackis sold in 1678 to Andreas Van Buskirk. Later, it became the boundary between the boroughs of New Milford and Teaneck. Since the Demarests were originally from France, it was called French Brook.

About a half mile south of the bridge on the east bank in Teaneck is a small monument marking the site of the old Lutheran Church. Most of the Lutherans were loyalists. The old cemetery that once stood behind the church on a high bluff overlooking a curve in the Hackensack River has been destroyed over the centuries by the river cutting into the bottom of the bluff and collapsing it.

T W O

The Long Retreat Continues

After the loss of Fort Lee and the escape over the New Bridge, in late November, 1776, the disheartening retreat continued. From Hackensack (November 18) to Newark (November 24), slowly on to New Brunswick (November 29) where Washington, always offense-minded, tried to rally his forces in a quick attempt at a stand. His limited artillery on the south bank of the Raritan traded shots with the British on the north bank. An unheralded young artilleryman named Alexander Hamilton was in charge of the cannon. On to Princeton (December 3), then to Trenton until stopped by the cold waters of the wide, swift Delaware River.

The few New Jersey militia troops that Washington had were far from being his best troops. The first enlistments of New Jersey troops had been sent north to help protect the northern border of New York state. The rest were a poorly-trained remnant of the Flying Camp that had been hastily organized to protect the western bank of the Hudson River. The best of the Flying Camp had been assigned more important duties and only the dregs were left.

As for the regular troops, few had anything resembling uniforms and many had thrown away their muskets and other paraphernalia in order to retreat faster. Their blankets, tents and entrenching tools had all been captured at Fort Lee. One British observer wrote, "no nation ever saw such a set of tatterdemalions."

At Newark, the panic had stopped and the battered army regrouped. Washington put his best men at the rear and began a slow retreat south. To follow an approximation of his route today, follow Route 27 from Elizabeth to Princeton, then Route 202 into Trenton.

Historians still argue about the reasons for the slow pursuit by British Generals Howe and Cornwallis. Both General Howe and his brother, Admiral Richard Howe, had been members of the Opposition Party in Parliament, opposed to the King's militaristic attitude when he named them in command of all his forces in

North America. In addition, the king had appointed them as peace commissioners and charged them with holding out an olive leaf to the rebels. However, all they were able to offer to the rebels was a promise not to prosecute them if they returned to the fold. As peace commissioners, they got nowhere, but it could help to explain why General Howe seemed to push his invasion of New Jersey just fast enough to let Washington escape before him. As one unhappy Hessian officer put it, "It became clearly evident that the march took place so slowly for no other reason than to permit Washington to cross the Delaware safely and peacefully."

Initially, it seems, Cornwallis's invasion of New Jersey was primarily to put Fort Lee out of commission, to make the Hudson River open to British warships. Fort Lee was not expected to cave in so quickly. It wasn't until Cornwallis saw Washington retreating so weakly that he began to follow. His initial orders from Howe were to pursue Washington only to the Raritan River.

Cornwallis wanted to catch Washington for a pitched battle on open, flat ground, the kind of battle that best suited European-style tactics. He remembered too well the retreat from Lexington and Concord with rustics shooting from behind every tree, wall, and barn. He also remembered Bunker Hill and the slaughter as British soldiers marched valiantly up the hill into the concentrated fire of dug-in Colonials.

Therefore, he approached every hill, barn, stone wall, and wooded area as if it sheltered a small army of tormentors. He wanted a battle, not a long-continuing skirmish.

Washington put out frantic calls for the Jersey militia to aid him in his hour of desperate need, and wrote to his brother about the militia: "They come, you cannot tell when, and act you cannot tell where, consume your provisions, waste your stores, and leave you at last at a critical moment." However, while very few joined Washington's retreating army, individual bands of militia were operating independently against the British and their local partisans in various parts of the state, especially in the Morristown area.

As peace commissioner, Howe offered amnesties to all who would sign an oath of allegiance to the King. People flocked in to accept the pardons, trying to side with the obvious winner, while few joined Washington. Desertions averaged about 100 men a day, steadily draining Washington's pitifully small army. From New Brunswick, Washington wrote: "The conduct of the Jerseys has been most infamous. Instead of turning out to defend their country, they are making their submissions [that is, accepting amnesties] as fast as they can."

An immigrant corset-maker from England who had joined Washington's little army sat down before the campfire in Newark one night, pulled up a drum and, using it as a desk, he began to write: "These are the times that try men's souls. The summer soldier and the sunshine patriot will, in this crisis, shrink from the service of his country; but he that stands it now deserves the love and thanks of man and woman." Thomas Paine's *Common Sense*, published a year earlier, had been instrumental in rousing the colonies to declare their independence. Now his second effort was to become another major contribution to American revolutionary literature. Paine left the army as soon as his manuscript was finished and rushed to Philadelphia to find a publisher. His *The American Crisis - Number One* was powerful in bolstering continuing support for the fight.

Slowly, Washington retreated, burning every bridge behind him and cutting trees to fall across the narrow roadways, staying just ahead of Cornwallis. One British officer wrote home in disgust, "The Rebels fly before us and when we come back, they always follow us; 'tis almost impossible to catch them. They will neither fight nor totally run away, but they keep at such a distance that we are always above a day's march from them. We seem to be playing at Bo Peep."

New Jersey's newly-elected legislature went into adjournment to allow every member to escape as best he could. The Continental Congress packed its bags in Philadelphia and fled to Baltimore, leaving Washington with "full powers to order and direct all things relative to the department and the operations of war." In forwarding this almost dictatorial power to Washington, Congress wrote to him, "Happy it is for this country that the general of their forces can safely be entrusted with the most unlimited power and neither personal security, liberty or property be in the least endangered thereby." They knew their man well.

One thing Washington did accomplish during the retreat: he developed a chain of spies he would benefit from for the next five years. One of the best was John Honeyman. His house, now privately owned, still stands near Griggstown. His neighbors all *knew* Honeyman was a rank Tory and most thought he was a sneaky British agent, to boot.

On December 1, with their enlistments expiring, 2000 of his troops from New Jersey and Maryland marched out of New Brunswick and went home. Washington sent urgent letters to General Charles Lee, urging this odd man to hurry and bring his force in to join the main army. Lee loitered along, waiting for Washington to make a final mistake so that Lee could take over his position.

Finally, after long delays, Lee started. He got as far as Bernardsville where he stopped to dally with a tavern owner's wife. A British party of roaming dragoons captured him. What looked at the time like another disaster turned out to be one of the best things to happen to the American cause.

Washington sent troops ahead to scour the Delaware for boats and remove all to the far side, except for those immediately needed, especially the big Durham boats. Then he brought his battered little army into Trenton and loaded their baggage and supplies into the waiting boats. Then, always the fighter, he turned his men around and marched back to Princeton to have one last go at the enemy. But his rear guard was already evacuating the college town. Reluctantly, he returned to Trenton and herded his men across to the relative safety of Pennsylvania.

Washington's last boats were leaving the Jersey shore when the first advance corps of Hessian jagers burst from the woods only "300 paces" away. They were greeted with an artillery barrage from the Pennsylvania shore that drove them back into the woods. General Howe arrived to take a look and a cannon ball landed so close it splashed mud all over him. He withdrew too.

Cornwallis, advancing on Trenton, split his army into two columns, one continued straight to Trenton, the other split off to Coryell's Ferry (present day Lambertville) to cross the river above Trenton and push Washington on to Philadelphia. But there were no boats. He scoured the river, even all its small tributaries, for miles in both directions. No boats. He sent a column down to Burlington. They, too, reported no boats to be found.

Back in Trenton, Cornwallis and Howe knew that many of Washington's enlistments expired on January 1 and fully expected his army to fade away over the winter. They lingered for a week, then decided to do what European armies usually did: go into winter quarters until spring. Cornwallis detailed his men to establish outposts at [reading from south to north] Burlington, Bordentown, Trenton, Princeton, New Brunswick, Elizabethtown, Newark, Hackensack, and New Bridge. Then he headed back to New York and boarded ship for a vacation back home with his wife and family.

Thomas Paine, having delivered his *Crisis* manuscript to a Philadelphia publisher, returned to the army. He summed up the situation: "With a handful of men we sustained an orderly retreat for near an hundred miles, brought off our ammunition, all of our field pieces, the greatest part of our stores, and had four rivers to pass. None can say that our retreat was precipitate, for we were near three weeks in performing it, that the country might have time to come in." Unfortunately, the country had not come in.

For Washington, on the far shore, the dark days continued.

T H R E E

The Short Road Back

For nearly three weeks, Washington had reeled back across the Jerseys, losing men, losing supplies, losing the man many felt was his best general. Now he was across the river and ice was forming over its swift current. If the ice froze thickly enough, quickly enough, it would bear the weight of men and cannon and he would have to begin the retreat again — that is, if he had enough of an army to retreat with. At least it was a temporary respite from running.

Immediately he began planning his return. He knew that he needed, quickly, some kind of positive news to rekindle the fire of independence. He needed something, especially, to get the January expires to re-enlist. He had one of his spies going into Trenton regularly and found that the presence of rapacious Hessians was converting many otherwise neutral civilians to the American cause. The mercenaries were stealing everything movable, from patriot and Tory alike.

Meanwhile, things were looking up a little. General Sullivan brought 2,000 of Lee's men into camp, General Gates showed up with 600 men from Schuyler's army, a battalion of German-Americans came in from Pennsylvania and Maryland, and 1,000 new enlistees came up from Philadelphia, swelling Washington's force to about 6,000 actives.

Also, back in New Jersey, other American forces were coming to life. Heath, moving down from Peekskill at Washington's request, tackled the Loyalist 4th Battalion of New Jersey Volunteers at Hackensack and came away with considerable stores. Another group of Continentals and New Yorkers hit a group of Loyalists near Leonia.

About 1,000 militia had gathered at Morristown. Fierce fighting broke out between militia and British regulars near Chatham and further east. When the Americans were reinforced, the British withdrew.

South of Trenton, militia from Philadelphia and from South Jersey harassed the Hessians under Count von Donop in Burlington. In fact, they greatly aided Washington without knowing it by drawing Donop out of Burlington and miles further south, away from Trenton, so that when Washington struck, Donop was too far south to help defend that town.

"It is now very unsafe for us to travel in Jersey," one Hessian officer wrote, "The rascal peasants meet our men alone or in small unarmed groups. They have their rifles hidden in the bushes or ditches and the like. When they believe they are sure of success and they see one or several men belonging to our army they shoot them in the head then quickly hide their rifles and pretend they know nothing."

To send a message to Princeton safely, Colonel Rall, in command at Trenton, used an escort of 100 men and a cannon to emphasize his problem.

But despite this, Washington still had no money and few supplies. His men were half naked, underfed, half frozen. And when enlistments expired on January 1, he would be back down to about 1,400 men. However, gradually, plans grew to go back across the river and surprise the Hessians at Trenton. The outcome of these plans would radically change the outcome of the war, and, quite possibly, the history of the world.

To help out, John Honeyman got himself captured by roving scouts and dragged before Washington, who interrogated this "British spy" personally and alone. Unfortunately, that night, the "British spy" managed to escape from his cell and get back across the river before the alarm could be raised. While in captivity he left with Washington a sketch of Trenton with all the Hessian forces identified and located.

There were several ferries in operation in 1776. The Trenton Ferry was just below the falls at the south end of town. Washington crossed on it going west. About eight miles north of Trenton were two ferries — Johnson's was licensed by New Jersey and carried traffic only to the western shore. McKonkey's Ferry was licensed by Pennsylvania and operated only east-bound. Further north, at what is now Lambertville, was Coryell's Ferry, operating both ways.

Today, there are two Washington Crossing State Parks, one in each state with a bridge connecting them. Start with the western one, because that is where the story of Washington's return begins.

Washington Crossing, Pennsylvania
Washington Crossing State Park
(215) 493-4076
Open Tuesday - Saturday 9-5, Sunday 12-5. Last tour at 4:00 during daylight saving time, 3:00 on standard time. Ticket for guided tour and admission to five buildings: $5.00, over 60 or autoclub member, $4.00, ages 6-18, $2.00. Under 6, free.

This 500-acre park is divided into two sections: the Thompson's Mill section is about a mile and a half south of New Hope, Pennsylvania on SR32. The Washington Crossing section is about five miles further south on SR32. A narrow bridge connects this section with the New Jersey Park. The park is administered by the Pennsylvania Historical and Museum Commission. Friends of Washington Crossing Historic Park are guides. Volunteers serve in many phases of the park including being tour guides.

Bowman's Tower
(215) 862-3166
Open Tuesday - Sunday 10-5, April to October, Saturday - Sunday 10-5 in October. Admission included in five building ticket.

A circular stone staircase takes you 100 feet up to the top of this tower on top of Bowman's Hill. For those less inclined to climb, an elevator takes one most of the way up. The hill provided Washington's army with a good observation post to keep watch across the river to make sure they were not being followed. Today, the tower is an excellent way to understand the terrain and get the lay of the land. The view, while wider, is probably much the same the Colonial lookouts would have seen — an agricultural country, dotted with homes here and there. Today, there are probably far more trees than there were then. (Trees get in the way of farming.) The army camped all along the land from the top of the hill down to the river.

A wildflower preserve with natural history exhibits is nearby, as are hiking trails and indoor exhibits. A memorial flag staff marks the graves of Washington's soldiers who died here during the encampment. It honors the first of America's "Unknown Soldiers."

Thompson-Neely House

Open weekdays 12-5, Sundays 1-5. About two miles north of Bowman's Tower on Route 32.

The oldest part of this house was built in 1702 by John Pridcock, the earliest settler in the area. He came here originally in 1684, built an earlier house, a grist mill and a trading post. By December 1776, two families were living in it — the Thompsons and the Neeleys. Now General William Alexander, called Lord Stirling, made it his headquarters. Several other officers, including Washington's cousin, Captain William Washington, and Lieutenant James Monroe, later our fifth president, moved in with Alexander.

Here, in the kitchen, Washington met with his leading officers to complete the plans for their return to New Jersey. The house is authentically restored and includes a hospital room. The barn has rifle slits for use during Indian attack. On the premises are ball-parks and picnic pavilions.

The Ferry House

Open Tuesday - Saturday 9-5, Sunday 12-5. No charge.

Samuel McKonkey bought the inn and ferry on the west bank in 1774. The present inn was built in about 1780 or 1790 on the foundations of the original inn. Only the foundation walls and a basement kitchen are part of the original. But this kitchen was probably used by Washington and his chief aides on the night of the crossing.

A Durham boat is on display outside the Ferry House. These were big husky boats used for generations in commerce on the river. They were built a few miles north near Riegelsville, Pennsylvania, by Robert Durham at the mouth of Durham Creek in Durham Village for the iron smelting operations of Durham Furnace. They were designed to carry iron ore, pig iron, and coal down river, and all manner of supplies upriver. They were very shallow draft and, even fully loaded, could float in about two and a half feet of water. About eight feet wide, they ranged up to 60 feet long. They were propelled forward by poling, not by rowing. They are obviously not the boat depicted in the famous painting. These were the boats that Washington insisted be gathered up from the eastern shore and hidden behind Malta Island just off the west bank.

Memorial Building

Open daily 9-5, Sundays 2-5. No charge.

This is the visitors reception center. There is a souvenir shop in the lobby with interesting wares in addition to the ones you would expect. Several museum exhibits share the corridors. The major part of the building is an auditorium with a huge copy of the famous painting by Emanuel Leutze, a German who never saw the Delaware River or a Durham boat. There is a ten-minute narration about the painting, shown at 9:00, 10:30, noon, 1:30, and 3:00. Free.

Also of interest:

Taylor House, built in 1816, was the home of a major businessman of the early 1800's in this area. Included in the five-building ticket.

Nearby:

Pennsbury Manor about ten miles away off SR13 in Morrisville.

(215) 946-0400

Tuesday - Saturday. 9-5, Sunday 12-5. Admission $5.00, over 60, $4.50, ages 6-12, $3.00.

Reconstructed 1683 country estate of William Penn. Manor house, outbuildings, gardens, picnic grounds. Demonstrate the high quality of living that was possible for some in the 17th century along the primitive Delaware River. Guides wear period costume that completes an authentic picture of eighteenth-century life.

The Crossing

The actual area where the army clambered into the boats is behind the Memorial Building. Any famous event must have some "famous words" connected to it. Years later, Henry Knox, Washington's artillery chief and a man of considerable girth, used to repeat what Washington said to him as they made ready to shove off: "Move your fat arse, Hank, but not too fast or you'll swamp the boat."

The embarkation area today features a wide pavilion with a reflecting pool and stone steps down to a river's edge lighted with tall lanterns. That Christmas night of December 25, 1776, there would have been nothing fancy. The mud along the river's edge would have been frozen solid. The river itself was ice-fringed, and ice floes tumbled past in the rapid current. The bare tree branches rattled in the wind.

Washington's plan, developed in numerous discussions with his staff, was a three-pronged operation. Washington would later learn not to attempt such complicated maneuvers that required close timing and interdependent movements in bad weather, on poor roads, with only rudimentary communications.

Colonel John Cadwalader with 2,000 men would cross the river further south to Bordentown and attack the Hessians there, to prevent their coming to Trenton's assistance. General James Ewing with 1,000 men would cross at the Trenton Ferry, where the Assunpink River entered the Delaware. He would take the high bluff on the south side of the Assunpink River to prevent the Trenton garrison from escaping in that direction. Washington himself with the rest of his army, about 2,400 men, would cross at McKonkey's and descend on Trenton from the north.

Sunset was about 4:30 on Christmas Day. The troops began to move about 4 o'clock. They moved south to the ferry hidden behind the screening hill that ran along beside the river. Company by company, they went over the hill into the boats manned by the

Marbleheaders of Massachusetts. The first brigade over moved rapidly inland and set up a screen through which no one was allowed to penetrate in either direction.

Christmas Day was cold, and as the day went on, grew colder...and colder...and colder. One young fifer, among the first across, wrote home that "we had to wait for the rest and so began to pull down the fences and make fires to warm ourselves, for the storm was increasing rapidly. After a while it rained, hailed, snowed, and froze, and at the same time blew a perfect hurricane, so much so that after putting the rail on to burn, the wind and fire would cut them in two in a moment, and when I turned my face toward the fire my back would be freezing. However, as my usual acuteness had not forsaken me, by turning round and round I kept myself from perishing before a large bonfire."

The snow fell in heavy gusts and slowed the men marching to the river. It slowed the manhandling of their few cannon into the boats. It slowed the boats crossing the river. And it slowed the men disembarking from the boats. By the time the last boat was emptied on the east bank, the operation had taken nine hours and was three hours behind schedule.

However, Washington made it across the Delaware that night. Cadwalader and Ewing didn't. Apparently, it took a Washington to do it.

Finally, everybody got across even though it took three hours more than had been allowed for. The schedule was already late as they climbed the steep embankment on the eastern shore, and they wasted no time getting underway as quickly as possible. General Greene with the main body took the upper, or Pennington, road with General Sullivan taking the river road. They would meet in the center of town. Washington accompanied Greene's column.

Washington Crossing, New Jersey
Washington Crossing State Park
(609) 737-0623
Open daily 8-8, Memorial Day to Labor Day; 8-4:30 the rest of the year. Parking: $3.00. Eight miles northwest of Trenton on State Route 29. Or Exit 1 on I95 then north on Route 29. Or U.S. Route 202 south to last exit before the Delaware River, then south on 29. Connects by bridge to Washington Crossing State

Park in Pennsylvania.

Route 29 and the Delaware Raritan Canal break the park into two sections that are joined by a covered walkway. The narrow little section west of the road and the canal are heavily wooded and have many park benches and picnic tables overlooking the river.

Washington Crossing State Park was established in 1912 and expanded in recent years under New Jersey's Green Acres program. It now includes 841 acres.

Visitor Center
(609) 737-9304
Open all year, Wednesday – Sunday 9-4:30.
This museum contains many Revolutionary War artifacts, mainly from the collections of Mr. Harry Kels Swan. Audio-visual shows, on the hour, explain what went on here. Guided historical tours of the entire complex start here.

A 140-acre Nature Center offers tours by appointment and provides plenty of room for hiking, biking, horseback riding, fishing, picnicking, and group camping (by reservation only). There is also the Washington Crossing Open Air Theater. A sloping hillside provides seating for some 900 people at summertime performances. For schedules and hours call: (609) 737-1826.

Get information at the Visitor Center for the numerous reenactments and other activities that take place in the course of the year. Each Christmas Day there is a reenactment of the crossing. In 1998, the reenactors had to walk across the bridge because, due to an extended drought, the river was too low to float the Durham boats. On Washington's birthday, local patriot organizations meet here to walk the route into Trenton. Visitors are welcome to join the march.

The Nelson House
This is a small house, on the west side of Route 29, near the river bank. It contains a small museum of historical exhibits and colonial crafts. It is headquarters for the George Washington Memorial Arboretum which has an assortment of native trees and shrubs indigenous to the area. The house is thought to be a section of an original ferry house. It is open only during the summer months. The house is operated and interpreted by the Washington

Crossing Association of New Jersey. For further information, call (609) 737-1783.

The Ferry House
(609) 737-2515
Open Wednesday - Saturday 10-12 and 1-4, Sunday 1-4. Free.

Johnson's Ferry House was built in 1737 and has been restored as a colonial inn and museum. Washington and his key commanders sheltered in this building for a final conference before heading off to Trenton. It is a small frame cottage originally built by a farmer of Dutch descent from whom it probably obtains its gambrel roof. The front is covered with "scalloped" shingles common to Dutch-built houses in central New Jersey. These are copies of the originals. During the Revolution it was a tavern as well as a ferry house. The downstairs rooms are fully furnished in colonial fashion. Upstairs are several small bedrooms that are as sparsely furnished as they would have been then. McKonkey, the ferryman from the Pennsylvania side, lived here after retiring from the ferry business.

One of the many odd little incidents that helped Washington in his comeback, without his knowing it, happened right in front of the ferry house, down by the river. On Christmas Eve, the night before Washington's Crossing, a group of about thirty American militiamen made an unauthorized crossing of the river. They were met by about forty Hessians and, after a brief skirmish, were driven back across the river. The Germans reported this incident back to headquarters, where it was thought that this was the American attack they had been warned of. Due to this, they let their guard down and were completely surprised by Washington thirty-six hours later.

Ferry House, Washington Crossing, NJ
Washington and several of his generals waited in Johnson's Ferry House as the landing progressed. The "scalloped" shingles are typical of early homes in this section of New Jersey.

The Flag Museum

This museum's main focus is a history of the American flag. Its most interesting exhibit is a large diorama of the Delaware Crossing and is an excellent way to understand the event. Smaller dioramas show the battles of Trenton and of Princeton. The building is a typical eighteenth century large stone building that was originally the barn for the Ferry House. Rest rooms are located here.

Continental Lane

Near the Flag Museum is a narrow little dirt path about five feet wide between little bands of trees. Supposedly, this is very close to the actual path the army followed when they stepped out from the boats. It's a nice little shady stroll running from the Ferry House to the Visitor Center. If you can ignore the blacktop roads on either side of the path, it is also a very moving stroll because it makes you feel that you really are walking in the footsteps of those giants who went before us.

Park Headquarters

Open Monday - Friday 9 to 5. Corner of Routes 546 and 579, (Pennington Road and Harbourtown Road).

This was the Bear Tavern where Washington is thought to have had a final conference with his key lieutenants, Greene and Sullivan, before they split up. After a brief conference, Greene went left to what is now Route 31, turned south and headed into the heart of town. Sullivan continued straight ahead on Pennington Road, which is also called Sullivan's Way, for the final part of its course. Now the old tavern is the park headquarters and visitor's information center.

The First Battle of Trenton

When Washington escaped across the river, the British went into winter quarters until spring time. By then, they expected, Washington's army would have melted away and the rebellion would be over. The outpost at Trenton was left under the command of Colonel Johann Rall, a very capable Hessian officer. He was the one who commanded the Hessian forces that reduced Fort Washington in northern Manhattan while Washington and Greene watched helplessly from the New Jersey shore.

Rall's superior, Count von Donop, took up quarters about nine miles south at Bordentown (sometimes then spelled "Burdentown"). However, in another of those odd things that helped Washington without his knowledge, Donop had been drawn south to Black Horse, and then further south to Mount Holly by militia under the control of American General Israel Putnam who was operating throughout South Jersey without Washington's knowledge. Without appreciating how he was helping, Putnam drew Donop so far south that he couldn't hear the guns of Washington's attack nor could he have gotten back in time to aid Rall.

An Officer of the Lossberg regiment wrote:

> We marched to Trenton and joined our two regiments of Rall and Knyphausen in order to take up a sort of winter quarters here, which are wretched enough. The town consists of about one hundred houses, of which many are mean and little, and it is easy to conceive how ill it must accommodate three regiments. The inhabitants, like those at Princeton, have almost all fled, so that we occupy bare walls.
>
> The Delaware, which is extremely rapid here and in general about two ells [90 inches] deep, separates us and the rebels. We are obliged to be constantly on our guard, and do very severe duty, though our people begin to grow

ragged and our baggage is left in New York.

Notwithstanding, we have marched across this extremely fine province of New Jersey which may justly be called the garden of America, yet it is by no means freed from the enemy and we are insecure.

This brigade has incontestably suffered the most of any, and we now lie at the advanced point, and thus as soon as the Delaware freezes over we may march and attack Philadelphia which is about 30 miles distant.

Trenton was not then the capital of New Jersey — Burlington and Perth Amboy shared that distinction — but it was at the head of navigation of the Delaware and a growing trade center. It was a semi-deserted village when the Hessians arrived, thus they had little problem finding warm lodgings for the Christmas season.

Rall had two shortcomings: he had nothing but contempt for the American army, and he liked to drink and play cards. Because of the first fault, he had not bothered to construct any fortifications around the little town despite being ordered to by his superior, Colonel von Donop. Several times he was warned that the Americans were making ready to cross the river and attack Trenton. His response was only, "Let them come."

Because of the second fault, he drank and played cards all of Christmas Day and almost all of Christmas night. During the evening, a local Tory passed him a note with the date and time of the planned American attack. Rall ignored it and just tucked it into his pocket. He, finally, made it to bed about 6:00 a.m., just two hours before the Americans struck.

Because his men knew their commander well, they also enjoyed themselves all night and didn't wake up until cannon thudded along King and Queen Streets. Washington's entire artillery battery — four small field pieces — had been set in place and were commanded by Washington's cousin William Washington, and the future president, James Monroe. One of the young artillerymen manning the battery was Alexander Hamilton.

The Hessians fell out into the street and managed to get two guns into action. William Washington and Monroe led a charge that put these guns out of action. Both were wounded. They were two of only four Americans wounded in the battle.

Meanwhile, Sullivan's men, coming into town from the south, met up with the Knyphausen Regiment at the Old Barracks and pushed them down to the Assunpink Creek at the southern end of town. About 400 Hessians escaped across the creek that was supposed to have been blocked by General Ewing's men, those who never made it across the Delaware that stormy night.

Because of the blinding snow, it was impossible to keep powder dry for use in muskets. Only the cannon were able to fire. When a message from General Sullivan told Washington this, the commander replied, "Tell General Sullivan to use the bayonet. I am resolved to take Trenton." Bayonets were fixed and the Hessians were forced into an orchard on the southeast side of town. Here they surrendered after Rall was fatally wounded. Later, the Tory's warning note was found in his pocket.

The battle lasted either thirty-five minutes or an hour and three quarters, depending on whom you believe. The last shot was fired about 9:30 a.m. Total American casualties were four men wounded. The Hessians lost 22 dead, 84 wounded, 868 taken prisoner and about 500 escaped.

Of great value to Washington were the stores captured: six double-fortified brass three-pounder cannon, three ammunition wagons, four wagons full of baggage, 40 horses, and about 1000 arms and accouterments.

Washington had had his sights set on Princeton and then New Brunswick after Trenton, but with the failure of Cadwalader and Ewing to join him, he felt unable to carry out the balance of his plan. Therefore, he bundled up his prisoners and scooted back across the river. It had been a long hard day, but one that completely changed the course of the war.

S I X

The Second Battle of Trenton

Back in the relative safety of Pennsylvania and after a good night's sleep, Washington learned that while Cadwalader had failed on Christmas night, he did get across the next day and found that the Hessians had deserted Bordentown and fled back to Amboy. On December 30, Washington called his army to order and offered them $10 each to reenlist for six more weeks. At first, none stepped forward. Washington addressed them again. "You have done," he said, "all I asked you to do and more than could reasonably be expected." He pointed out the victory they had won, and the greater good they could do. Then, he asked again for them to step forward. Slowly one man shrugged, then stepped forward, then another, until gradually every one of them stepped up and reenlisted. Two days later, they crossed the river again and did what Washington enjoyed most — went on the offensive. Bringing all his troops in from surrounding areas, Washington now had some 5,000 men and forty captured cannons in Trenton.

Back in New York, all were in shock. British and Hessian troops poured into town from New Jersey. Cornwallis canceled his vacation reservations, gathered his troops and marched back towards Trenton.

The two armies made first contact part way between Princeton and Trenton. There had been a thaw, and the marching armies had churned the road into mud. The British pushed ahead, slowly, because Washington's men, under General Hand, split into small units and harassed the Redcoats every step of the way. It was like the march back from Concord and Lexington all over again. It took eight hours for Cornwallis to move forward just eight miles.

Finally, in late afternoon, Cornwallis pushed into Trenton. Washington's troops escaped over the Assunpink bridge to the high ground to the south. Cornwallis made three attempts to cross the bridge. Each time they were met by a solid blast of cannon and musket fire that forced them back. Then, quite content with the progress that his force had made that day, Cornwallis ordered, "Rest for now. We'll bag the fox tomorrow."

That night they rested in Trenton, watched the fires burning on top of the hill and listened to the sound of Washington's men fortifying their entrenchments.

Trenton

The Battle Monument

Open Wednesday - Sunday 10-12, 1-5, all year. The monument is in the middle of downtown at the juncture of Warren and Broad Streets, where the American artillery had been set up.

A statue of Washington stands atop this 150-foot, Roman-Doric tower, viewing the scene of his most important victory. An elevator goes to the top where one gets a fine view of the surrounding terrain. This is the highest spot in Trenton, one of the points where von Donop instructed Rall to build an entrenchment. It's also where William Washington and James Monroe put their guns into action to dominate the village. You can follow the two main streets as they diverge into the heart of the town. You can see the approaches to town and the scenes of the most vigorous action. It's from this point also that William Washington and James Monroe launched their bayonet attack on the Hessian gunners.

The monument, designed by John H. Duncan, is of white granite from Maine. Philadelphia artist Thomas Eakins did the bronze plaques on the monument. At the time of the Bicentennial they were taken off for cleaning. They were appraised at the Corcoran Gallery at more than $150,000. The statues on either side of the door represent John Russell of John Glover's Marblehead regiment, who ferried the troops across the river, and private Blair McClenachan of the Philadelphia troop of light horse.

St. Michael's Church

On the east side of Warren Street, just past Perry Street.

Behind this church, Rall, in a last-ditch maneuver, tried to rally his troops into something resembling an orderly formation and make a counterattack, but American cannon fire broke up his attempt. The American fire was so furious that the Hessians broke and ran, ending in an orchard at the end of Warren Street.

The Old Barracks

Barrack Street (609) 396-1776
Open daily 10-5. Admission $6.00, seniors and students $4:00.
Under 6, free.

In 1758, at the height of the French and Indian War, barracks for British soldiers were built in several cities to try to stop the complaints about barracking British soldiers in private homes. This is the only one remaining. Over the years, it has been occupied by British, Hessian, Continental, and Tory troops. Today, it is a museum simulating eighteenth century officers' quarters. It is well done and gives the feeling the troops have just left for formation. Costumed guides lead tours. At the time of Washington's capture of the town, it was occupied by Hessians.

Trent House

15 Market Street (609) 989-3027
Open daily 12:30-4:00. Admission $2.50, seniors and autoclubs
$2.00, Under 12, $1.00.

Built in 1729, this is thought to be the oldest house in Trenton. It was built by William Trent, after whom the town is named. It was occupied by Hessians at the time of the battle. The home has been beautifully maintained and is well worth a visit. Even though not directly connected with Washington, he probably spent time in it on his numerous visits to Trenton.

Lewis Morris, the first royal governor of New Jersey, lived in this house for several years. General Anthony Wayne lived here while negotiating with the Pennsylvania Line troops who mutinied at Morristown in 1781.

If you're lucky, the cupola on top of the house will be open and you can see across the Delaware River to the west. Views of the city are partly blocked by tall modern buildings. It was Ewing's target, if he had managed to get his troops across that night.

Also of interest:
New Jersey State Museum

205 West State Street (609) 292-6464
Open Tuesday - Saturday 9-4:45, Sunday 12-5. Donations are
requested.

The main museum has three floors of exhibits and offers films, concerts, and lectures. **The Planetarium** offers changing night time programs. For further information: Trenton Convention and Visitors Bureau, Lafayette Street at Barrack Street.

(609) 777-1771

Douglass House

Intersection of Front and Montgomery Streets, Trenton.
Open Monday - Saturday 10-4, Sunday 1-4, all year.

This house was built on South Broad Street about 1766 (where the Lutheran Church now stands). On the night of January 2, 1777, Washington met with his major commanders to consult on what to do next after the British had driven them back to the Assunpink Creek. Here, he spelled out his plan to leave his camp-fires burning and go the back way to Princeton.

The Battle of Princeton

The men at the top of the hill, tending the fires and making the noises were only a small part of Washington's army. As soon as it was dark, Washington led the majority of his force off to the east into the darkness on tiptoe. They found a little-used road described by one of Washington's spies and headed north for Princeton. This was literally a blood-in-the-footprints march through the snow. A fast-dropping thermometer had turned the muddy trail to edges sharp enough to cut through the rags wrapping the feet of many of the men.

As day broke they emerged at the edge of the village of Princeton, near the stone bridge over Stony Brook. Washington paused beside the Friends Meeting House beside the brook and sent General Hugh Mercer ahead with about 400 men to demolish the bridge to slow down Cornwallis when he returned from Trenton, as Washington knew he would.

When Mercer's men got out into the open, they could see the backs of two regiments of Redcoats under the command of General Mawhood, heading for Trenton. The British saw Mercer's men at the same time and wheeled about to attack.

A sharp battle quickly developed with the British charging in a bayonet attack. Mercer's outnumbered troops fell back in confusion and Mercer himself fell, pierced with many bayonet wounds.

Just when it looked like the British were winning, Washington galloped in between the opposing armies and, waving his sword, shouted his men forward. Momentarily, smoke covered the battlefield. When it cleared, the men expected to find Washington fallen, but there he was, still urging them on. Quickly, they brought their greater number to bear and beat the British back, finally sending them fleeing in a rout. The Americans chased them for a couple of miles, but Washington, knowing that Cornwallis was only nine miles away, and would have heard the sound of the cannons, called them back and turned them into town.

Other Redcoats crowded into Nassau Hall, the main building of the College of New Jersey (now Princeton University). Washington pulled his cannon up and fired into the building. The British quickly surrendered. Legend has it that one ball launched from Alexander Hamilton's cannon went through a window and into a portrait of King George III, decapitating him. This ominous sight caused his soldiers to surrender.

The battle lasted no more than thirty minutes and cost the Americans only about forty killed and wounded. The British lost more than eighty-five killed and wounded and about 300 prisoners.

Pushing his prisoners ahead of him, Washington headed north out of Princeton as quickly as he could. His next target was to have been New Brunswick where he knew a large store of supplies was kept, along with a heavy war chest supposedly worth some 70,000 pounds sterling of hard money. However, his troops had been marching all night, had fought two battles in as many days and were exhausted. He needed a safe refuge to lick his wounds and rebuild his army. He spent a night or two in the little village of Pluckemin, then headed north into the hills for Morristown.

In just nine days, Washington had surprised and defeated two of Howe's strongest outposts. Obviously, he could snap up any of the others any time he wished. Howe called all his extended army back into New York, keeping control in New Jersey of only a thin line from Perth Amboy to New Brunswick. Washington, with a beaten and defeated army operating against overwhelming odds, had inflicted on the enemy two severe defeats and had freed almost the entire state of New Jersey from a far superior army.

Watchers in both Europe and America suddenly awoke to the fact that this war was far from over. And that the Americans had a real leader.

This nine-day campaign is still considered one of the finest military campaigns in world history. After the war, the British historian George O. Trevelyan wrote, "It may be doubted whether so small a number of men ever employed so short a space of time with greater or more lasting results upon the history of the world." It sounds like Winston Churchill describing the Royal Air Force after the Battle of Britain.

Princeton

Princeton Battle Monument

Princeton is about ten miles north of Trenton on SR 583 and US Route 1. The Battle Monument will be on your left shortly after you have crossed a small stream. It is about a mile southwest of the town of Princeton, on Mercer Street.

The Princeton Battlefield State Park occupies about 85 acres on both sides of Mercer Street and is open to wandering, picnicking, and wedding photography. The Battle Monument is a 50-foot block of Indiana marble with four white Greek columns. The high relief carving shows a figure of Liberty rallying Washington and his troops.

The Battle Monument is on the hill where the battle ended. American soldiers killed in the battle are buried behind it, British soldiers off to the side.

Mercer Street did not exist in 1777, but this was the high ground of the area and both armies were trying to take it. On the east side of Mercer Street, standing alone in the middle of the battlefield, is the Mercer Oak. This gnarled old tree was young when the wounded American General Hugh Mercer was placed beneath it. He had been bayoneted several times and was obviously beyond help. When the short, sharp battle was over he was carried to the nearby Clarke home, where he clung to life for six days before dying.

Near the tall flagpole, a plaque marks the burial place of British soldiers who died in the battle. A gravel path behind the monument leads to a grove of tall evergreens that mark the burial sight of Americans slain in the fight.

The Thomas Clarke House

(609) 921-0074
Open all year Wednesday - Saturday 10-12 and 1-4, Sunday 1-4. No fee.

Thomas Clarke, a local farmer, built this house about 1770 and lived there until his death in 1802. The house was off to the left of the main battle and was used as a hospital after it was over. American General Hugh Mercer, one of Washington's better leaders, was wounded in the battle and died in this house six days later.

The house is furnished as it was during the Revolution and exhibits weapons, paintings and maps of the battle. The house and nearby grounds are being developed as a working farm of the period. This is a great improvement since the first time I saw the battlefield, when most of it was covered with a crop of cabbage.

When this scraggly old oak was a young sapling, the wounded body of General Mercer was laid under it until the battle ended. He died at the Clarke House several days later.

The Friends Meetinghouse

Go south on Mercer Street from the Battle Monument to the first intersection and turn left on Quaker Road just before reaching the old stone bridge over Stony Brook. The Meeting House is a small stone building on your left at the end of a long drive.

Quakers were early settlers in New Jersey. In fact, William Penn led a Quaker settlement here before the one in Pennsylvania. Quakers settled in Princeton as early as 1696. Their first meeting house (1709) was destroyed by fire, as was the second one. This, the third building on the site, was built in 1758. The front porch is a later addition.

This building served as a hospital after the battle. It is still in regular use as a meetinghouse. In the walled cemetery are many Revolutionary War period graves. As you enter the cemetery, on your right, is a marker indicating that Richard Stockton, a signer of the Declaration of Independence and one of New Jersey's wartime leaders, is buried in this cemetery. No one knows where.

Nassau Hall, the centerpiece of Princeton University, was then its only building. It was used by the American army, the British army, American army mutineers, and the Continental Congress during the revolution.

Nassau Hall

Nassau Hall is not open to the public on an everyday basis. It is a part of Princeton University. Guided tours of the University start with Nassau Hall.

Nassau Hall was built in 1754 and was the first and only building at the college for fifty years. During the war years it was occupied by whichever army happened to be in town. In 1781, it was occupied by the mutinous Pennsylvania Line when it marched out of Jockey Hollow.

After the main part of the Battle of Princeton was over, a small group of British soldiers holed up in Nassau Hall but were taken prisoner. Later yet, Nassau Hall was occupied by the Continental Congress from June to November 1783. During a special session at that time, the Congress voted its personal thanks to Washington for his service during the war. It was here that Congress, presided over by New Jerseyan Elias Boudinot [see Boxwood Hall, page 98], received news of the Treaty of Paris, officially ending the war.

The towering cupola was added several years after the Revolution. Cannonball damage can still be seen on the back of the building near the roof line.

Also of interest:
Bainbridge House
158 Nassau Street (609) 921-6748
Open Tuesday - Sunday 12-4 pm. Free.

Captain William Bainbridge, born in this house in 1774, was a hero in the fighting against the Tripoli pirates and later a commander of "Old Ironsides," the *USS Constitution*, during the War of 1812. The house, built in 1766, has been restored as a museum. It was occupied by British General William Howe during Washington's retreat across the Jerseys in the fall of 1776. After the battle of Princeton, the Bainbridge family was forced to leave town due to their Tory leanings. Today, it is headquarters of the Historical Society of Princeton. Get brochures and maps here for walking tours of the town.

Princeton University
(609) 258-3000
One of America's oldest and most distinguished institutions of higher education. Free tours of the campus are available Monday-Saturday at 10:00, 11:00, 1:30, and 3:30. Contact Maclean House, 73 Nassau Street, a big yellow building next door to Nassau Hall for further information.

Morven

55 Stockton Street, between Library Place and Bayard Lane.
Open Saturday 10-1 and Wednesday 10-12 all year. Free.

Richard Stockton and his wife Annis built this house in 1754. She was the sister of Elias Boudinot, a leading New Jersey patriot, of whom more later. Stockton was a New Jersey representative to the Continental Congress and was a signer of the Declaration of Independence. He was captured by the British, imprisoned, severely treated, and forced to sign a loyalty oath. He was the only Signer to recant. He died before the war ended, with many thinking he died as a direct result of this brutal treatment.

In 1776, Cornwallis used it as his headquarters. Before he arrived, Stockton and his family buried the family silver and other valuables in the extensive garden. After the battle of Princeton, when the British troops were forced to flee, they first looted and defaced the house and partially burned it.

In the summer of 1783, when Congress was sitting in Princeton, it was the headquarters of Elias Boudinot, then president of the Congress. Word arrived from Europe that, finally, a peace treaty had been signed with the British declaring the United States to be a free and independent country. Thus, Elias Boudinot was the first official President of the United States, and Morven was its first "White House."

The name Morven comes from the home of Fingal, third century king of the northwestern Caledonians. It was mentioned in a supposed translation of a poet of the time, Ossian, who wrote:

> *Sons of Morven, spread the feast,*
> *Send the night away with song.*

Annis Stockton liked that sentiment and named her house from it.

The house was much smaller in Annis' day. The front piazza was added in 1790 and the second stories on both wings were added by a later Stockton.

It remained in the Stockton family until 1945 when it was purchased by the state and was designated as the official residence of New Jersey's governors. Its five acres of gardens, lawns, and ancient trees give it a majestic character. Probably no other state executive mansion has the historic background and character of Morven.

Rocky Hill

Rockingham

(609) 921-8835

Normally open Wednesday - Saturday 10-12, 1-4, Sunday 1-4, but now closed for restoration. Call to learn status. Free.

Five miles north of Princeton on County Route 518.

In 1783, Congress was meeting in Nassau Hall in Princeton, to avoid the throngs of veterans who had been besieging them in Philadelphia trying to collect back pay. Here they debated the peace treaty with England and wanted Washington nearby for consultations. Because Princeton itself was so crowded, Congress found him a house in Rocky Hill, about five miles away.

Judge John Berrien had built the two-story white clapboard house in 1710. He died during the Revolution and his widow wasn't able to sell it because of the war. She was happy to find tenants for it. Her six children were all grown and gone, so she had plenty of space available. The Washingtons moved in. It was to be the last of his many headquarters.

While here, Washington wrote a final "farewell address to the troops." While it was sent to West Point to be printed and distributed, Washington is said to have stood on the narrow upstairs back porch to read it to a small gathering of his soldiers. This is not to be confused with his Farewell Address to his officers, delivered a few months later at Fraunces Tavern in New York.

The house has been moved from its original site not once but three times. The furnishings are of the Revolutionary period but are not original to the house. Martha's bedroom downstairs and his office upstairs have been restored to their original appearance.

E I G H T

The First Winter in Morristown

The Trenton-Princeton campaign not only changed the course of the war, it established Washington as a brilliant military leader both in America and abroad. Years later, after General Cornwallis had surrendered to Washington at Yorktown on the Chesapeake, Washington invited all of the vanquished enemy generals to a formal dinner at Yorktown. At the dinner, General Cornwallis made this toast to honor Washington: "When the illustrious part that your Excellency has borne in this long and arduous contest becomes a matter of history, fame will gather your brightest laurels rather from the banks of the Delaware than from those of the Chesapeake."

Having fought three successful battles in less than ten days, and made an all-night forced march in the snow, Washington's troops were badly in need of rest and sustenance. He chose to rest a day or two and then take the forty-mile march to the village of Morristown, safely behind a protective mountain chain.

The Watchung Mountains extend south from the Passaic River in a 45-mile stretch almost to the Raritan River. At the southernmost point, they make a short sharp hook to the northwest. There are two parallel "mountains" to the chain with a pleasant valley in between. At their highest, they're only about 600 feet above sea level. But their eastern slopes are precipitous, and both mountains present sharp, difficult climbs for the foot soldier. To their west, the Passaic River creates a third barrier, behind which in another set of steep hills, lies Morristown. The Watchungs provided another advantage: from their eastern crests the entire Jersey plain lay bare to Washington's watchers. Any British troop movement would be quickly spotted.

The remnants of his little victorious army rested in Pluckemin then crept into Morristown on January 7, 1777. The pleasant little green in the village center was bordered by Samuel Arnold's Tavern, three churches, the schoolhouse, courthouse and jail.

Washington chose the tavern as his headquarters. Arnold's son, Jacob, was the colonel of Morris County's first company of light horse and was paymaster for the militia. The building was on the southwest corner of the green and was demolished in 1886.

Morristown then was only a few buildings and a couple of taverns, but boasted three churches with spires. The town green was an open field where horses, cows, pigs, and sheep grazed. The churches, courthouse, and jail gave some semblance of civilization to the little hamlet. There were about 250 residents who were swamped by the twenty-times-that-many soldiers who moved in on them.

Morristown was like any number of other tiny clusters of homes in northern New Jersey at the time, but this one was destined to become the military capital of the new nation for several years. It was already a center of militia activity led by Jacob Ford, Jr.

To the east, the steep little Watchung Mountains were protection from the British thirty miles away in New York. Watchers on these mountain ridges could see out over the farmland to detect almost any military movement. It also gave Washington good access to the "highways" leading to the nation's capital in Philadelphia, in case Howe moved that way — or up the Hudson if the British chose to go that way.

The troops, a little over 5,000 in number, were barracked in private homes and barns throughout the area. However, to confuse the British, Washington kept moving them from place to place so that not even the locals knew how many there were. To cap the matter, he had his adjutant general draw up a set of false returns showing a total of more than 12,000 men present and capable. Then he "lost" this where he was sure a British spy would easily find it.

One incident is typical of Washington's outlook. One of his young officers burst into his office one day demanding permission to arrest a man he knew to be a British spy. Washington calmed him down and told him, "Better to make a friend of him, buy him a meal, and tell him we have 20,000 men here."

They drew on the produce of the land to heal their wounds and refill their bellies. The hills west and north of the village were rich in iron ore, and Washington took the opportunity to encourage the producers of this valuable material.

One of the local leaders, Jacob Ford, Sr., had already petitioned Congress for financial help in building a powder mill near his big new home east of the village. Washington, functioning as his own chief supply officer, encouraged him.

Disease turned out to be Washington's biggest enemy that winter in Morristown. At the time, a small-scale epidemic of smallpox, "the greatest of all calamities," was moving throughout the nation and would continue until a few years after the war was over. Smallpox became a factor in every major campaign from then on. Both sides were accused of what we would now call bioterrorism, that is, the use of disease as a weapon.

Smallpox had decimated Benedict Arnold's army near Quebec. It had hampered the British occupation of Boston. Now it began to sweep Washington's army in Morristown. Washington himself was immune due to an attack of the disease when he was a young man. Now he struck back. Long before many medical men agreed on the value of vaccination and against the fears that much of the population had about it, he ordered all soldiers to be inoculated. The three churches became hospitals, filled with sick and dying, but gradually the dread disease was conquered within the ranks of the Continental soldiers. New recruits were inoculated and held outside of camp. This added four weeks to the recruitment cycle but was worth it. The army survived and was physically fit when fighting weather returned.

There are many historic sites in and around Morristown. For information on them, see the section "The Bitter Cold Winter in Morristown," beginning on page 83.

Washington's Strategy Develops

Due to the ever-present shortages of food, clothing, and military supplies, small units of the army constantly prowled the neighboring hills and valleys, by day and by night, purchasing where possible, taking where necessary. British and Tory units were doing the same, except rarely purchasing. This was the beginning of the guerrilla warfare that would consume northeastern New Jersey for the next six years. This became, probably, the most fought-over section of the nation during those years. While there were only two major pitched battles here, Springfield and Monmouth, the skirmishing was constant.

Washington set up a great semicircle of outposts, a mixture of Continentals, state troops and militia, stretching from Sandy Hook in the south, around through Middlebrook and Morristown, up to West Point and across the Hudson through Fishkill, and down through Westchester County into southwestern Connecticut. This would become the ring that would expand or contract according to British movements.

The British, at the center of the ring, would need food for humans and animals but had only Long Island to draw from easily. Today an army needs gasoline to move, then it needed hay. Each horse required fourteen pounds of hay each day, plus ten pounds of oats and four pounds of straw. The British would have to break through the ring to obtain these necessities. Washington gave instructions to remove as many supplies as possible from the inner ring so that the British would have to go further for them, and could be harassed every inch of the way, out and back. This situation would remain in effect for the rest of the war.

On December 20, at the depths of the darkest day in the new nation's short history, Washington had written a long letter to Congress. In it, he condemned many of the problems that Congress forced upon him, such as short-term enlistments, the low average ability of too many of his lower-ranking officers appointed by Congress or by the states, the absence of cavalry, and other shortcomings. Congress panicked and fled from Philadelphia to Baltimore, then responded on the last day of the year. They made him absolute dictator for six months, giving him all that he had asked for in his letter.

It's a major measure of Washington's greatness that here was an absolute dictatorship placed in his hands, and he turned it down. He did take advantage of it to get all the things he had asked for. He spent the next several months in Morristown rebuilding his army, improving his officer corps, enlisting soldiers for three-year terms in units that were truly continental, and not organized by states or localities. They came in slowly but steadily. Gradually, throughout the spring in Morristown, he built his army up into an effective force that would remain loyal to him in the bitter years ahead.

As the spring weather warmed, the British maintained small units in Amboy and Brunswick. In May, Sir William Howe sent a sizeable body of troops from Staten Island into central Jersey, in the Raritan Valley. His main hope was to draw Washington down from the mountains and into a set battle on the flatlands, the kind of battle that his troops were best at, and Washington's were not trained for.

Washington moved south but remained within the protective shelter of the Watchung Mountains. However, he knew that his job was to keep an army alive and to avoid exactly the kind of battle that Howe wanted. His main job was to keep an "army-in-being."

He knew also that given time, the huge British army would take much more food and fodder from local farmers than his small army would, thus slowly turning the local residents against the British and to support for the rebels.

In the spring of 1777, it looked to Washington as if British General Howe was planning to attack Philadelphia by crossing New Jersey. So Washington moved troops south to put them in front of the British. His main body went into encampment north of the Raritan River, about five miles from the crossing to New Brunswick, in an area known as Middlebrook, now a part of Bound Brook.

Washington used this encampment several times during the

war. In 1779, while troops were here, Washington established winter quarters at the Wallace House in nearby Somerville. Efforts are being made to restore the area and erect a monument. At present there is little to see.

In June 1777, Howe made his move, bringing 18,000 men into position between New Brunswick and Somerset. Washington sent General Nathaniel Greene to attack the British rear guard and General William "Scotch Willie" Maxwell to nearby Metuchen. Howe tried to circle Maxwell to seize the passes through the Watchungs in Middlebrook. This would cut off Washington's safe return to the hills.

Maxwell was in no position to send a warning to Washington so he attacked Howe's forces, knowing the sound of gunfire would alert Washington to the danger. Washington retreated to a position of safety that also was a strategic threat to Howe.

Sharp skirmishes took place around Middlebrook, one of them big enough to be called the Battle of Short Hills (not the area presently known as Short Hills in Essex County, but in Scotch Plains in Union County). Earlier in the spring, the New Jersey militia, fleeing from a British cavalry unit in this area, had lured them into Ash Brook Swamp where the horses floundered. Meanwhile the militia walked away laughing.

Now, Washington with about 6,000 men came down out of the mountains. Howe, with about 18,000 men, had given all signs of pulling back onto Staten Island when he suddenly swung about and attacked, hoping to catch Washington off guard and cut him off from his escape route back into the Watchung Mountains.

Washington's troops were saved by one of New Jersey's more colorful characters: Major General William Alexander, better known as Lord Stirling. He was a wealthy landowner from Basking Ridge who claimed to be the successor to the Scottish title, "Earl of Stirling." While England never recognized his claim, most Americans did. Even Washington called him "My Lord." On this occasion, his 1,700 troops put up such a strong resistance to Howe's superior numbers that Washington was able to withdraw safely back into the hills. A marker at the entrance to Ash Grove Country Club gives the details of the battle.

In late June, Howe pulled back from his positions in New Jersey. A year earlier, the British had conquered New Jersey. Now there was not a single British soldier in the state. Washington had made a clean sweep.

Green Brook

Washington Rock State Park

Take County Route 529 west off SR22, to the top of First Mountain of the Watchung Range.

This was one of several outlooks at the top of the Watchungs from which Washington's scouts could keep watch on the plains below. Even on a misty day, lookouts could see for miles. Driving up narrow Route 529 gives a good idea of the steepness and rugged character of the Watchungs, and what a good military barrier they made.

Looking out over the plains, remember that there are far more trees today than there were in the 1770's. Most of the plains were farm lands from which almost all of the trees had been cleared. Roads then were all unpaved dirt, from which huge clouds of dust would rise from the boots of marching soldiers. A military movement could be detected from miles away.

Plainfield

Drake House

602 West Front Street (908) 755-5831
Sunday 2-5 by appointment.

This little house, squeezed between big homes on a typical suburban street, is a little hard to find but worth the trip. It's a typical farmhouse of the 1770's, with a few outbuildings remaining. It has been preserved by, and is now operated by, the Plainfield and North Plainfield Historical Society.

There's a connection here with Washington, but nobody knows for sure what it is. Nathaniel Drake, owner in 1777, had a 17-year-old daughter, Phoebe, whose writings tell us Washington was a visitor. Others claim that he stayed here while planning his strategy for the Battle of the Short Hills. However, the Battle of the Short Hills all happened so fast, it seems unlikely that any of it was planned in advance.

T E N

Where is Howe Going?

News trickling down from the north was not good. General Burgoyne with a strong force was moving down Lake Champlain. Fort Ticonderoga, supposedly impregnable, fell without a shot being fired. Word came that in New York City, Howe was loading troops and horses aboard ships. Was he heading up the Hudson to help Burgoyne? Or was he heading south to attack up the Delaware River and take Philadelphia, the capital of the new nation?

Washington believed strongly that Howe would make some kind of strong movement up the Hudson to help Burgoyne. That's what he would have done in Howe's position. The Hudson was navigable for big ships as far north as Albany, which was obviously Burgoyne's target. Washington, therefore, began moving troops north, but not too far north, just in case Howe should make a fast move toward Philadelphia. He accompanied the first units to move north.

Washington's spies told him that Howe's transport ships were loaded and ready to sail. Finally, on July 24, 1777, they sailed — out of the harbor and south along the Jersey shore. There was only one place he was likely to go — Philadelphia. Washington left a strong detachment in the Hudson Highlands, just in case Howe was feigning a move on Philadelphia and would return back up the river. Then he slowly moved the major part of his troops south and west to be ready for a British move up the Delaware River. But Howe's ships, taking their time, sailed right past the Delaware Capes and disappeared out to sea.

Instead of coming up the Delaware River, Howe came north through Chesapeake Bay and unloaded his army at Head of Elk. To protect Philadelphia, Washington interposed his army when Howe tried to cross the Brandywine River in Delaware. With a sweeping flank movement, Howe rolled Washington back in a severe defeat and went on to seize the capital city with little opposition. The Continental Congress again fled to safer parts.

When Benjamin Franklin, in France, was told that Howe had captured Philadelphia, he answered, "Or Philadelphia has captured Howe." Franklin was right again, as usual.

Washington spent the winter of 1777-1778 in the cold of a little Pennsylvania village, Valley Forge. Here, with the help of a Prussian volunteer, Baron von Steuben, he would teach his new army how to march and maneuver as an army should. In the long run, the American army that froze and drilled hard all winter long while the British lived high on the hog in the big city was to prove victorious when the springtime came.

Wayne
The Schuyler-Colfax House
2343 Paterson-Hamburg Turnpike
This house is on the west side of the northern part of the Turnpike. It is closed for renovation and will reopen in the spring of 2003. For further information, call the Wayne Township Historical Commission at (973) 694-7192.

Around 1700, Arent Schuyler, a young trader recently arrived in America from Holland, built a one-room stone house at the side of an Indian trail, overlooking a placid but strong-flowing small river. Twenty years later, he added a second room to the little building. He would later become quite wealthy from copper found accidentally on his main farm in New Barbadoes (now Kearney and North Arlington). He would be the first American to own a steam engine, imported from England to pump water out of his copper mine.

Washington spent the nights of July 11-13, 1777, in this little two-room house, according to research done by Susan Deckert of the Daughters of the American Revolution. The neighborhood must have been rather scant for this little building to have been the best one that Washington could find to quarter in.

In 1783, William Colfax, a Virginian officer in Washington's Life Guard, married Arent Schuyler's granddaughter, Hester, and went on to build an imposing addition to the little two-room house. Later, General and Martha Washington would visit the house for the christening of young George Washington Colfax. Little George's brother, Schuyler Colfax, would grow up to be vice president under President Grant.

Nearby:

While in Wayne, visit the Dey Mansion, (see page 105) and a few miles southeast in Towaco is the Henry Doremus House. (see page 101)

Oakland
The Hendrick Van Allen House
Route 202 and Franklin Avenue
Open the first and third Sundays of each month, from 1-4. Closed July, August, December, and January.
Take Route 287 to Exit 58 on Route 202. North on Route 202 two blocks.

The Ramapo Valley Road (today's Route 202) was a back way north from Morristown to West Point, used quite often by the army and by New Englanders going to or from their home territory. Washington left the Schuyler-Colfax House (see above) on July 14, 1777, and led his troops north over one steep ridge and down into another valley. That night he stayed at the Van Allen house and continued moving his troops north "over extremely deep and miry roads" the next day.

The house was built in the early 1700's by Hendrick Van Allen as part of his 200-acre farm. During 1778 and 1779, British and Tory raids were so frequent in central Bergen County that the county court house was moved from Hackensack to this house for safety reasons.

The house is now the headquarters the Oakland Historical Society which, with the help of the local Women's Club, saved it from destruction.

The Battle of Monmouth

In September 1777, Howe captured America's capital city, Philadelphia. Having done so, he found he was no further along in winning the war than he had been before. Until Washington's army was wiped out, the war wouldn't be won.

To make Howe's situation worse, in October he learned that his colleague General John Burgoyne had just surrendered his whole British army to the colonials at Saratoga, partly because Howe had not sent troops north to help him.

King George III was not pleased. To make him even more displeased, in February 1778, France officially recognized the United States as an independent nation and declared war against Britain on America's side. Spain and Holland soon followed France's example, happy to help kick their old enemy, the British, at a time when it was heavily engaged elsewhere. This changed the entire nature of the war from a small colonial uprising to a widespread World War.

In March, George III said to his war minister Lord North, "It was a joke to think of keeping Philadelphia." In April, General Howe was ordered home and his successor, General Henry Clinton, was ordered to take his army back to New York. The whole nature of the war would change.

Washington and his army, 10,000 strong, had spent the winter in Valley Forge, cold but active, while Howe and his army were in Philadelphia, warm, cozy, and wrapped up in a gala social season. Washington had been joined by a short, stout Prussian who could barely speak English, Baron von Steuben. Cussing in three languages and working through interpreters, he soon whipped Washington's troops into line.

He started with a model troop of 100 men and trained them in military drill, maneuvers, and discipline. These 100 then each took 100 men to train. Soon the whole army was marching, countermarching, and maneuvering to drum beats and bugle calls as a unified mass for the first time. When General Clinton pulled out of Philadelphia in June 1778, the army that chased him was far different than the one he had chased the previous fall.

Steuben was later to write to an old Prussian friend about the difference between the American soldier and the European one: "In the first place," he wrote, "the genius of this nation is not in the least to be compared with that of the Prussians, Austrians, or French. You say to your soldier, 'Do this' and he doeth it, but I am obliged to say, 'This is the reason why you ought to do that' and then he does it."

Clinton pulled out of Philadelphia on June 18, but Washington knew about the move in advance. One of his spies was a laundryman who sent word that the British officers had just ordered their laundry sent back quickly — washed or not — indicating they must be about to leave.

Clinton crossed the Delaware at Gloucester, New Jersey, and headed north toward New Brunswick with a supply train of 1,500 wagons that stretched twelve miles long. One local witness wrote: "The great amount of materials to be transported, and the number and variety of troops, made its movement very slow, as the army was four days and nights passing through Haddonfield. Bakeries, laundries, hospitals, and smith shops were on wheels, as well as boats, bridges, magazines, and medicine chests."

The female camp followers were the greatest annoyance to the residents of the place. "They would enter the dwellings and premises of the people, carry off such things as they might select, and if interfered with would insult the owners by lewd conduct and obscene language." Local residents drove their cattle to secret hiding places and buried their valuables including even breakable furniture.

The British line was unwieldy, and New Jersey militia forces were adept at breaking down bridges and causeways and felling huge trees across roads. In the first six days Clinton was able to move only about thirty-five miles to Allentown. In those same six days, Washington's pursuing army covered fifty-seven miles.

At Allentown, Clinton decided not to risk a dangerous crossing of the Raritan River and turned east to follow a route through Englishtown and Monmouth Court House (now Freehold) to Sandy Hook.

Up until now, he had been able to use parallel roads to move his troops on one and his baggage on the other. Now he had to put them both in one column. He put about 4,000 troops in front, then his long baggage train, then another 6,000 troops as a rear guard, under Cornwallis, his best general.

Washington, meanwhile, was having managerial problems. General Charles Lee, who had been captured at Bernardsville a year and a half earlier, had been swapped for a British general who had also been captured during a dalliance with a young lady. Technically, Lee was still second in command in the American army, so Washington offered him command of the advance corps.

Lee felt that the retreating British should not be attacked. If anything, they should be assisted in leaving New Jersey as rapidly as possible, "over a bridge of gold," he said. He felt the American rabble could not stand against the disciplined British army and contemptuously turned down the offer of command. After this irritating, time-wasting wrangle, Washington gave the command to young General Lafayette with instructions to harass the enemy but not to engage fully unless an unusually good opportunity exposed itself.

As they neared the British rear, Washington added more and more troops to Lafayette's advance corps. When Lee saw how big it was becoming, he changed his mind and demanded that he be given the command. Reluctantly, Washington agreed.

It was one of those stifling New Jersey summer days, a 3-H day — Hazy, Hot and Humid — temperature in the high nineties, perhaps over 100 degrees. The armies in their hot woolen uniforms and heavy packs (the British packs weighed sixty to eighty pounds) moved about as fast as present traffic moves on a hot summer Saturday at a Garden State Parkway toll plaza. Later, when the "butcher's bill" was totted up, it was thought that almost as many men fell because of the heat as because of enemy fire.

Except for the heat, historians still can't agree on what happened that day. The battlefield has only been under official development since the 1976 Bicentennial celebration. Amateur historians with metal detectors are still finding new facts about exactly where the long battle was fought. Here is approximately what happened.

Lee, now leading almost half of the army, started forward early in the morning before the heat became brutal. At 11:30, Washington was in Englishtown, dictating a letter to Congress to tell them that he had high hopes of catching up with the British before they could get out of reach. Just before noon, he heard cannons boom and the rattle of musket fire. He galloped forward.

Lee had made contact with what appeared to be only about 1,500 or 2,000 of Clinton's rear guard. He began the attack. But General Cornwallis, commanding the British rear, turned his whole force around and counterattacked. The suddenness of his strike stalled Lee and caused him to pull back some of his units. Other groups saw them go and thought a general retreat had been called. Lee gave conflicting orders or, for some units, no orders at all. Quickly the careful retreat became a rout with troops falling all over themselves to get away as fast as they could.

Washington and his staff, coming up, encountered the first of the panicky men and demanded to know what was happening. Galloping forward he found Lee. "What is the meaning of this?" he screamed. Lee could only sputter, "Sir...Sir..." It is said that Washington swore so hard at Lee that "the very leaves on the trees trembled." It was one of the very rare occasions when he totally lost control of his fiery temper.

Washington took over the command and, only minutes before the British were upon them, ordered some fast troop movements and rallied the men back into the lines. Alexander Hamilton, writing after the battle, said, "I never saw the General to so much advantage. His coolness and firmness was admirable.... A general rout, dismay and disgrace would have attended the whole army in any other hands but his."

Lafayette wrote, "General Washington seemed to arrest fortune with one glance. His presence stopped the retreat.... I thought then as now that I had never beheld so superb a man."

The American troops rallied with a discipline and with precision maneuvers that would have been impossible a year earlier. They halted Cornwallis's advance. Clinton turned his entire rear guard — half of the entire British army — back, but it was a narrow battlefield and only limited troops could engage at one time. In the sweltering heat, the impetus swept back and forth for the whole afternoon. It developed into the longest single battle of the entire eight years of war.

The American army was in constant movement, maneuvering to meet each new British charge, and doing it as professionally as any European army could. Hamilton later said that it was the first time he had fully realized the value of military discipline while under fire. The crusty old baron had done his work well.

At one American artillery squad, the wife of one of the gunners was helping her man by carrying cool water from a nearby spring. Her man was hit and fell, she put down her pitcher, picked up his ramrod and filled his place at the gun. Thus was "Molly Pitcher" born. There's an arrow now pointing to the spring where she, supposedly, performed her heroic work.

By nightfall both armies were exhausted. When the blessed cool of night came, they slept on their arms. But, early before dawn, there was a turn of the tables. Clinton pulled a Washington, packing up his army and creeping away under cover of night. By daylight he was gone. His retreat from Philadelphia had been a disastrous move. He lost some 500 men in the battle at Monmouth and nearly 2,000 during the flight, many of them fell to New Jersey's brutal heat. Many others took the opportunity to desert into the beautiful New Jersey countryside.

That night, lodged at the Village Inn in Englishtown, General Lee asked for a court martial, "to clear his good name." Washington, staying at the same inn, obliged. The court martial was held in Morristown, and Lee was found guilty. His punishment was to remain out of the army for one year. Instead, he resigned from the service.

Lee always maintained that he was leading a skillful withdrawal to better positions and should not have had his command taken away from him. Many historians now agree with him. Many others don't. The question is still being argued.

Freehold
Monmouth Battle Monument
70 Court Street, opposite the Monmouth County Historical Association.
The granite monument consists of a cylindrical block on a triangular base supporting an eighty-five foot shaft.

The battle of Monmouth was fought over gently rolling farmland, divided by hedgerows. The Visitor's Center looks out over the same lush fields.

The statue on top is "Liberty Triumphant." The original statue on top was destroyed by lightning in 1913. Its replacement was modeled by Mary Anderson, a popular actress of the time. The five bronze tablets at the base represent scenes of the battle. It is said that 25,000 people gathered for the original dedication in 1884.

Monmouth Battlefield Visitor Center

Route 522, northwest of Freehold (908) 462-9616
Open daily, 9-4. Free.
Park area open 8-dusk every day.

The battlefield at Monmouth is still very much in the condition it was in 1778. It is gently rolling hills, basically farmland. It hasn't succumbed to urban or suburban sprawl, unlike Trenton or Springfield battlegrounds. It is pretty countryside, especially when the leaves have turned in autumn.

The Visitor Center provides a display that shows troop movements during the battle. It is a good introduction to the events of the day. The Center is nicely placed at the top of Comb's Hill so that most of the battlefield is visible from this spot. During the battle a Virginia artillery battery under General Greene occupied this site and did heavy damage to the British who occupied the row of trees to the right.

Intensive archeological work, both amateur and professional, is being conducted on the battlefield and new knowledge is changing previous thinking about many aspects of the battle. One interesting display shows a variety of recovered musket balls that have been misshapen in different ways by hitting different objects.

On the last weekend in June, the Battle of Monmouth is reenacted here. Among the amenities at the Center are rest rooms, a snack bar and a gift shop, open weekends during summer months. Many picnic tables are spread through the grounds.

Also of interest:

Just north on Route 522 is Owl Haven Nature Center, operated by the New Jersey Audubon Society. This includes natural history exhibits, displays, and a bookstore. Throughout the battlegrounds are walking and riding trails. A map is available at the Center.

Craig House

Route 9 and Schibanoff Road (908) 462-9616
Open mid-April to mid-November, Sundays, 1-4. Call in advance to make sure it's open. Donations accepted. This house is quite apart from the rest of the battlefield park. It is just west of Route

9 at its corner with Schibanoff Road. Watch for signs for Craig House.

The Craig House was built in 1710 with a major addition in 1754. It was occupied by Alexander Craig and his wife and their eleven children. It remained in the Craig family until the 1940s. It's a typical Dutch frame house, in the middle of farm land, just as it was then. Of the six rooms, only three are open to the public.

The house survived the Battle of Monmouth and was used as a hospital by the British during the fight and by the Americans after the battle was over. An electronic map of the area shows the movements of the troops of both sides and helps to explain the confused movements of the two armies.

The battle raged around the Craig House, on the eastern edge of the present park area. The small wing dates back to the early 1700's, the large part to 1754.

Couvenhoven House
150 Main Street (732) 462-1466
Immediately east of the Route 9 overpass on the south side of Route 33. Open June to October, Tuesday, Thursday, and Sunday 1-4, Saturday 10-4. Adults $2.00, children $1.00.

A small house on this site was built in 1706. It was greatly enlarged in the 1750's by William and Libertje Couvenhoven. It was Clinton's headquarters before and during the battle of Monmouth. The Couvenhovens, knowing the British and Hessian tendencies to appropriate whatever wasn't nailed down, moved all of their furniture into hiding before Clinton arrived.

Clinton, however, was very persuasive in saying that such a move was unnecessary and, really, was an affront to his honor as a general. He assured the Couvenhovens that their furnishings would be safe and even sent his own soldiers to bring it all back. The next morning, Mrs. Couvenhoven found that all of her belongings had been plundered and stolen, and all their horses and cattle had been taken as well.

The period furnishings of the house today are based on a 1790 inventory of the household. In the kitchen, there is a rare set of four matching Jersey slipware plates. The master bedroom on the second floor is highlighted by unusual wall paintings that were discovered during restoration, when twenty-nine layers of paint were removed.

Also of interest:
Monmouth County Historical Association Museum and Library
Open Tuesday - Saturday 10-4, Sunday 1-4. Library open Wednesday - Saturday 10-4. Admission $2.00, seniors $1.50, ages 6-18, $1.00. (732) 462-1466.
The museum houses decorative arts, paintings, furniture, folk art, and toys; most of them made in New Jersey. There are changing exhibits, battle artifacts, and a research library for genealogists. The Society owns and operates four historic sites in Monmouth County.

Battleground Arts Center
35 West Main Street (732) 462-8811
The center features classical and popular concerts, a symphony orchestra, live theater, and art festivals. There are special youth programs and the Monmouth Repertory Company.

Tennent
Old Tennent Church
445 Tennent Road, County Route 3. Just north of intersection with County Route 522 (Monmouth Battlefield Road). Open Saturdays and Sundays or by appointment.

Old Tennent Church

Reverend William Tennent was one of a group of evangelical Presbyterian and Dutch Reformed preachers who sparked the Great Awakening among American churches in the middle 1700's. He and most of his parishioners were strong supporters of the American forces during the Revolution. He served this church for forty-three years and is buried under the center aisle. He died just over a year before his church became part of a battlefield.

Parts of the battlefield are visible from the slight rise the church sits on. Almost all of it is visible from the steeple, where some of Washington's officers were stationed to keep him posted with intelligence of the battle. At one point, he met with some of his key personnel at the door of the church.

Inside, the church is calm and peaceful in its stark eighteenth-century Presbyterian plainness. The pulpit rises high in front, with its sounding board overheard to make the Lord's message audible to all.

The church was used as a hospital after the battle and many veterans of the battle are buried in the church yard. British Lieutenant Colonel Henry Monckton, the highest ranking officer on either side killed during the battle, is buried here. Local tradition says that cannonballs were dug out of walls and were found on the grounds as late as 1913.

Englishtown
The Village Inn
Corner of Main Street and Water Street. This 1726 inn, complete with outbuildings, has not been open to the public recently. There are no regular hours at present. Visitors can arrange to see the Inn by writing to the Battleground Historical Society, P.O. Box 161, Trenton, N.J. 07763.

The night of the battle, lodged at the Village Inn, General Lee asked for a court martial "to clear his good name." Washington, staying at the same inn, obliged. The court martial was held in Morristown, and Lee was found guilty. He resigned from the service.

That summer, Washington reflected,

> It is not a little pleasing nor less wonderful to contemplate that after two years maneuvering and undergoing the strangest vicissitudes that perhaps ever attended any one contest since the Creation, both armies are brought back to the very point they set out from, and that which was the offending party in the beginning is now reduced to the spade and pickaxe for defense.

The British were penned into New York City and the patriots occupied the rest of the country.

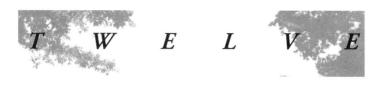

T W E L V E

The Hot Summer Simmers On

As the British escaped from New Jersey, back to the safety of Staten Island and Manhattan, Washington moved his troops up to New Brunswick to rest them and to celebrate the second anniversary of independence. From there, he moved them slowly north, expecting Howe's next move to be up the Hudson River.

Early in July, Washington was headquartered at the old Paramus Church (replaced on the same site in about 1800 by the present church on Route 17) for several days. James McHenry, one of his aides wrote,

> The General, receiving a note of invitation from a Mrs. Prevost to make her Hermitage, as she called it, the seat of his stay while in Paramus.... At Mrs. Prevost's we found some fair Refugees from New York who were on a visit to the Lady of the Hermitage. With them we talked and walked and laughed and gallanted away the leisure hours of four days and four nights, and would have gallanted and danced and laughed and talked and walked with them till now had not the General given orders for departure.

Washington undoubtedly joined in the gallanting, walking, talking, and dancing.

Ho-Ho-Kus

The Hermitage

335 North Franklin Turnpike (201) 445-8311
Tours Wednesdays and two Sundays per month. Call for details.
There is a small admission fee. From Garden State Parkway: Exit 165, head west on Ridgewood Avenue into downtown Ridgewood. Right at stoplight at Maple Avenue. Go north about 1.5 miles to stoplight at Franklin Turnpike. Ho-Ho-Kus Inn, also dating from

Revolutionary times, is right ahead of you. Left onto Franklin Turnpike, about half a mile on the left.

Washington apparently stopped here more than once, and he and Lafayette are both known to have slept here. It looks like the height of Victorian gimcrackery — fanciful bargeboards under the eaves, steep sharp-gabled roof, diamond-paned windows, but it started as a solid four-square Jersey Dutch brownstone in 1750. It underwent its transformation to Gothic Revival a hundred years later. During the Revolution, it was one of the proudest homes along the old Albany Post Road. At that time it was owned by a British army officer named Prevost. He was stationed in the West Indies, and his wife Theodosia stayed here alone.

Most of Bergen County was a no-man's land. British control reached up from the south as far as the English Neighborhood (present Englewood). American control extended south from New York state to an outpost at nearby Paramus Church. Periodically, the Americans raided to the south, or the British raided to the north. The Hermitage was never far from the war.

Mrs. Prevost, despite being the wife of a British officer, was often helpful to the American cause. In fact, New Jersey's Chief Justice Robert Morris had pleaded in the courts for leniency in applying enemy property laws against the Prevost estate in light of her help to patriots during the first British invasion of the area in 1776.

Aaron Burr, then one of Washington's more effective young officers, also stayed here, and, after Theodosia Prevost became a widow in early 1780, he became a regular visitor. The story is told that Burr was in command of patriot troops in Westchester County. At the end of the day, when his men were bedded down for the night, Burr would gallop his horse to the Hudson River. A waiting boat would ferry him across to what is now known as Alpine Landing. A waiting horse would carry him at speed to The Hermitage. He would spend the night here, then gallop back at sunrise to join his troops as they mustered for the day. A small stone house, a couple of miles up Franklin Turnpike, was a tavern during the Revolution, and supposedly Burr stopped there regularly for refreshment on his way to or from The Hermitage. Later, Aaron and Theodosia married and had a daughter, also named Theodosia.

In September, 1780, The Hermitage would again come into the news. Benedict Arnold's treachery at West Point was uncovered.

While he escaped, he left behind his wife, Peggy Shippen Arnold, and their six-month old son, Noddy. Peggy, hair disheveled and in her dressing gown, screamed, shrieked, fell to her knees and carried on in what was, apparently, the biggest role of her young life.

The act continued for two days. She played her part so well it was written up in the *New York Post* and the *Pennsylvania Gazette*. Washington was so full of sympathy for the poor young girl, he sent her with a guard back to her family in Philadelphia. Her second stop on the way home was at The Hermitage.

Years later, Burr reported that Theodosia had told him, "As soon as we [she and Peggy] were alone, Mrs. Arnold became tranquilized and assured Mrs. Prevost that she was heartily tired of the theatricals she was exhibiting." According to her story, Peggy admitted that "she had corresponded with the British commander and that she was disgusted with the American cause...and that through unceasing perseverance, she had ultimately brought the general into an arrangement to surrender West Point."

Shortly after, Washington would be staying at the nearby DeWint House in Tappan, New York, during the trial and execution of British Major John Andre, Arnold's co-conspirator.

In the mid-1800's the solid old red sandstone Jersey Dutch structure was Victorianized. Now it is classic Gothic Revival Victorian.

In the first half of the 20th Century, The Hermitage went into a long sad decline. It was dark and gloomy and almost unoccupied. To the kids of the neighborhood it was known as "The Witch House." When its final lonely occupant died, it was willed to the state, and the long slow climb back up began, promoted by a group known as The Friends of The Hermitage.

Today, The Hermitage celebrates its Victorian heritage more than its Revolutionary one. The Friends of The Hermitage offer Dickensian Christmas gatherings, Victorian tea parties, fashion shows, and twice-yearly crafts shows.

The Hot Summer Turns Even Hotter

Washington left a few troops, including a cavalry troop, at New Bridge and went on up into Westchester County in New York State. In late July, American militia made a sweep down into what is now Hudson County, raiding as far as the town of Bergen (now Jersey City). They captured some 300 cattle and 80 sheep along with other staples and valuables taken from known Tories.

In late September, the British responded, in spades. Several thousand troops landed at Paulus Hook and surged up through the English Neighborhood and into New Bridge. Five thousand red-coats camped between Liberty Pole (Englewood) and New Bridge. General Cornwallis set up headquarters at what is now the corner of Teaneck Road and New Bridge Road in a house torn down just a few years ago.

General Howe himself moved north up the Hudson. Washington wrote that "The design of these movements is proba-bly a forage and a gathering of stock, but it may also be something else."

Among the American troops in northern New Jersey was a reg-iment of light horse under Colonel George Baylor, a well-thought-of commander and the son of a close friend of Washington's back home. As the British moved in, he led his troop north along the Hackensack River almost up to the New York border. They bivouacked one night in a couple of barns owned by a Jersey Dutchman known to be a Tory.

The farmer managed to get word of his visitors to the British at New Bridge and, shortly after dark, four regiments under General Charles Grey headed north. Grey had a reputation as being a hard, ruthless man. He gloried in his nickname, "No-flint" Grey. He would rather use a bayonet than fire a musket. About midnight, he descended on the quiet barns, and the "Baylor Massacre" took place. In his report to Cornwallis, he estimated fifty killed out of the 120 rebels. His estimate was probably high.

River Vale

Baylor Massacre Park

Rivervale Road is a main north/south road through the northern part of the county. The park is on Red Oak Drive where it meets River Vale Road. Operated by the Bergen County Park Commission. Open all year.

In the 1960's the Bergen County Historical Society sponsored an archeological dig at a Revolutionary-era tanning yard. Remains of six American soldiers were found. A serene memorial park now occupies the site. It's a pleasant place to sit or stroll for a few minutes. The sturdy old Jersey Dutch stone house to which the barns belonged is across River Vale Road and up a little way.

Meanwhile, on a larger scale, the war had been changing. In February 1778, France had declared war on England, and, in September, The Netherlands signed a treaty of "amity and commerce" with the new United States. These two events changed the war from a small colonial one to being a world war, to be fought by the British on many fronts.

In December, a British expeditionary force of 3,500 troops moved south and captured Savannah, Georgia. From then on, most major activities would be in the south. Washington remained in New Jersey, keeping the major part of the British army penned into New York.

As fall approached, Washington arranged his troops in smaller encampments from Connecticut through Westchester County and into New Jersey. It would be easier for these small units to acquire adequate food and supplies from the nearby countryside than it would be for one or two large encampments. The largest encampment was at Middlebrook, so Washington made his headquarters nearby.

Somerville

The Wallace House

38 Washington Place (908) 725-1015
Open Wednesday - Friday, 9-12 and 1-6, Saturday, 10-12 and 1-6. Sunday 1-6. Closed holidays. Donations accepted. Reservations required for parties of 10 or more people.

Wealthy Philadelphia tea merchant John Wallace purchased a small house and farm in 1775 from Jacob Hardenburgh, pastor of three local Dutch Reformed churches. It's the small wing of the present building. He then proceeded, slowly, to have a large addition added to it. Due to the war, Wallace couldn't get away from Philadelphia, and construction crawled along. It was just finished in December 1778, when he learned that the Washingtons needed a temporary home while the troops were in the Middlebrook encampment.

Washington moved in immediately and wrote to Martha to come north. Then he was called to Philadelphia to meet with the Congress for six weeks. When he returned to the Wallace House, Martha was with him. They rented the house for $1,000 and stayed here until June 3. During this time they became close friends with the Reverend Jacob Hardenbergh and his wife. Their manse was just across the street.

The Washingtons spent winter and spring of 1779 in John Wallace's new house in Somerville and became quite good friends with their neighbors across the road.

It was here that Monsieur Girard, France's first ambassador to the United States, caught up with and was introduced to Washington.

The Wallace family moved in shortly after the Washingtons left. Later, their daughter married the son of Jacob Hardenburgh, across the street.

The Old Dutch Parsonage
65 Washington Place (908) 725-1015
Open Wednesday - Friday 9-12 and 1-6, Saturday 10-12 and 1-6. Sunday 1-6. Closed holidays. Donations accepted.

This solid brick house was built in 1751 as the home of the parson of three local Dutch Reformed churches, Frederick Frelinghuysen, the first of many Frelinghuysens to serve their state and their country, even down to the present. In addition to serving his pastorates, he trained young men to become ministers in a school he established in a large room on the second floor. Three of his students were living in the house when Frelinghuysen died at age twenty-seven, leaving behind his wife, Dina, and two small children.

One of these young students, Jacob Hardenbergh, then seventeen, proposed to the twenty-eight-year-old widow. Three years later, after he was ordained, they married and moved into the old parsonage, to which he had been called. They were resident there when the Washingtons moved in across the street.

Hardenbergh was active in the internal conflicts in the Dutch Reformed Church in America and was one of the leading members of the *coetus*, or evangelical branch of the church. His little school was the seed from which grew Queens College, a Dutch Reformed seminary for the education and ordination of ministers in America. In 1785, he was named president of the institution. This later became Rutgers University. He was also an ardent patriot during the Revolution, as were most Dutch Reformed clergy.

The house was originally directly across the street from the Wallace House but was moved in 1914 so that new railroad tracks could be laid through its site. It contains exhibits of local history and lifestyles, and early American crafts. One of the interesting things about it is the third floor smokehouse. Keeping the meat up there was much safer than having it downstairs or in an adjacent outbuilding when an army full of expert pilferers was in the neighborhood.

The local chapter of the Daughters of the American Revolution was instrumental in saving this house and restoring it to its original appearance. Now it and the Wallace House across the street, are both operated by the New Jersey Division of Parks and Forestry.

Pluckemin

The Boylan House

Pluckemin is on Routes 202-206 a few miles north of Somerville. Many of the houses are old and much of the town is on the National Historic Register. The large area where General Knox had his artillery park is now occupied by a sprawling apartment project. The Boylan House is a red building housing a real estate office on the east side of the main street across from the 1852 Presbyterian church.

After the battle of Princeton, Washington had headed his tired but triumphant army north for Morristown. When they reached

Pluckemin, a tiny village in the shadow of the southern tip of the Watchung Mountains, they could go no further. Washington called a halt, and they spent a couple of days recuperating before going the last fifteen or so miles to Morristown.

Now, two years later, in February 1779, the Washingtons were living in the Wallace house in nearby Somerville. Andrew Compton, then owner of the Boylan House, and several neighbors, perhaps instigated by General Knox whose artillery was parked behind the house, held a "Grand Alliance Ball" to celebrate the first anniversary of the entry of France into the war on the patriot side. Naturally, the Washingtons were invited as guests of honor.

Washington, however, wrote back to Compton, "I should be happy to indulge your request of being present at Pluckemin on the 18th. But I do not think it can be done with propriety, especially under the present appearances of a movement among the enemy, which your letter, concurring with the intelligence received from Captain Stokes indicates. The enemy may think our attention too much engaged in the exhibition of that day, and may be encouraged to some enterprise on that account."

Maybe this was just to throw off the enemy if they were reading Compton's mail, but the ball was honored by the presence of the General and his wife. They danced the night away.

Henry Knox, whose cannon were parked in Compton's back yard, wrote an account to his brother: "We had above seventy ladies, all of the first *ton* [fashion] in the State and between three hundred and four hundred Gentlemen. We danced all night — an elegant room. The illuminating, fireworks, &c., were more than pretty." In the field behind the house, near his guns, Knox had erected a temple, or frame, of thirteen Corinthian arches, 100 feet in length, each arch had an illuminated painting of the Revolution.

This house in the little village of Pluckemin was built in 1751. It has been "modernized" or "restored" many times over the years. It now houses a real estate agency. That gives new meaning to the phrase "open to the public."

Raids and Counter-Raids

The year 1779 continued with Washington's major problems being those of finance and supply. In June, Spain joined the war against England without making any change in the war in New Jersey. The only notable action came in August when Washington, then headquartered at New Bridge, sent Colonel Henry "Light Horse Harry" Lee on a nighttime raid on the British outpost at Paulus Hook (now Jersey City).

It was a simple plan of attack, but everything that could conceivably go wrong did. Paulus Hook was a point of land opposite the southern tip of Manhattan. At high tide, it was almost an island, as the marshy lands surrounding it filled with water. A causeway was the only entrance to it.

Lee's attack was timed for low tide, just before dawn, but his troops (numbering only 300) got lost, maybe by getting directions from a Tory guide. After wandering in the heavily forested steep backslope of the Palisades, they finally found their way to the causeway about two hours late. The tide was coming in, making the causeway almost impassable.

Despite the adverse conditions, Lee attacked. His men scaled the defensive walls and quickly conquered the surprised garrison, most of whose members were up in Bergen County, raiding near Closter. Then Lee headed back to meet the boats that were to carry his troops up the Hackensack River to safety. Unfortunately, the boats had waited for him to show up two hours past his appointed time and had then departed, thinking the operation had been called off.

Lee then headed back the way he came, on the one road leading to English Neighborhood. At the same time, the British who had been raiding to the north started back to Paulus Hook on the same road. The two forces met by surprise just where the road turns west to Liberty Pole and New Bridge. Fortunately, Washington had sent out reinforcements to meet Lee, and the British were routed. Lee got back to New Bridge safely. Lee's raid accomplished little but made great news that cheered the morale of the patriots in a year when little else did.

The Bitter Cold Winter in Morristown

Washington brought his army back to the safety of Morristown for the second time on December 1, 1779. Jacob Ford had died, leaving a widow and four young children. She invited Washington and his immediate staff to make the new Ford mansion his headquarters. He agreed and sent for Martha to stay with him. The main part of the army, now more than 12,000 strong, camped about five miles down the road at a place called Jockey Hollow.

That winter was the bitterest of the entire century. Twenty-eight blizzards swept the mountainous area, piling snow feet deep on the camp. The temperature dropped to zero, and stayed there. From there, on January 23, it plummeted to seventeen degrees *below* zero on a British Army thermometer, still New York City's unofficial low temperature record. Even the brackish water of New York harbor froze solid — solid enough for the British to haul cannon across it with oxen. The weather was so bad that Martha couldn't get here until the first of March.

It was bad in a fine new house in Morristown, but it was far worse a few miles south in Jockey Hollow.

Morristown
Washington's Headquarters/Ford's Mansion

Washington Place
(973) 539-2085
The Historical Park consists of the Historical Museum and Library, at the rear, and the Ford Mansion, or Washington's Headquarters. Enter through the Museum. Admission is $4.00. Under 16 and Golden Age Passport are free. Open 9-5 daily. The Headquarters tours

Ford's Mansion was Washington's headquarters for seven months during the worst winter of the century. Martha came north and lived here with him.

depart from the Museum every hour from 10-4. The Library hous-
es some 40,000 manuscripts and 20,000 printed works dealing
with the Colonial and Revolutionary periods. It is open by
appointment. To give yourself plenty of time to enjoy the Museum
and Headquarters, allow at least two hours.

There are many things that make a visit to the Ford Mansion delightful, but, primarily, it is the way it is treated as a home occupied by living, breathing human beings, rather than as a temple filled with antiques. The docents bring a special warmth to the tour. The typical little printed legends outside of each room don't describe the furnishings within, they describe what the room was used for, and by whom.

One night in the bitter winter of '79-'80, it was so cold, the only warm place in the big house was Mrs. Ford's spacious kitchen, so all 20 plus residents huddled together here in front of a blazing fire

This is a large Georgian house, with large rooms and many of them. The docents do a wonderful job of explaining how the Widow Ford and her four children, George Washington with his wife and eighteen aides, plus visiting messengers and dignitaries, all survived together for nearly seven months. There are only four rooms on the ground floor. Washington complained for months that he had no kitchen of his own. When he finally had boards cut to build an outside kitchen, he wound up giving them to General Henry Knox to build an extra room for his pregnant wife onto the side of an existing small home.

Note especially the big kitchen where on one bitter evening in February, it was so cold that Washington, his military "family," and the Fords all clustered in front of the fireplace all night because it was the only place in the house that was the least bit warm.

Furnishings are not only of the period, but about eighty percent were there when the Washingtons were. The room on the second floor where the Washingtons dwelt is an example of how crowded they were. Here they ate, slept, did the General's business, met with distinguished visitors, and even relaxed a little.

One report by an officer's wife, writing home from Morristown, tells that "almost every afternoon they went riding with the general."

She may have thought it was for fun, but it was really Washington's surveyor's eye at work. He learned the local terrain firsthand, wherever he happened to be. He knew he might have to fight on that ground someday.

The Schuyler-Hamilton House
5 Olyphant Place
Open Tuesdays and Sundays, 2-5.
This 18th century farmhouse was the residence of Dr. Jabez Campfield, a well-known Revolutionary War surgeon. General Philip Schuyler, his wife, and his pretty daughter Betsy, were quartered here while he conferred with Washington at the headquarters. One of Washington's dashing young aides living at the Ford Mansion was Alexander Hamilton. He courted the vivacious Betsy while she was here and later married her at the Schuyler mansion outside of Albany, New York. It was quite a step up for the penniless young man from the West Indies who was very sensitive about his illegitimate birth.

The home where General Philip Schuyler, his wife, and daughter Betsy were bivouacked on a visit to Washington. Betsy was swept off her feet by dashing young Alexander Hamilton, a Washington aide. Later, they married.

The home has been saved by the Morristown Chapter of the Daughters of the American Revolution, and is staffed by its volunteers. The house contains a number of interesting relics of the period. The good doctor's medicinal herb garden is still maintained in the backyard.

Fort Nonsense
From the village square, take Western Avenue left onto Ann Street, then a right turn onto the road leading uphill. Go all the way to the top.
Washington put his troops to work building entrenchments on top of the highest hill in town. His troops called the fortification Fort Nonsense because they saw no reason for it, and because it was just "make work" to keep them out of trouble. However, as you

look out over the hills to the east, you can appreciate how the observer can see almost all the way to Manhattan, where the British were. In the 1770's, when no roads were paved and military operations were carried on primarily in good dry summer weather, any major military movement would stir up a cloud of dust visible from here. Thus, Fort Nonsense made a lot of sense.

There is little to see at the site, except for the magnificent view. There are markers which show the general layout of the earthworks.

Also of interest:
Morristown has many other sites of interest, unrelated to Washington and the Revolution. Self-guided walking tour guides are available. Visit the Historic Morris Visitors Center at 6 Court Street for further information.

Acorn Hall
68 Morris Avenue
Open March - December, Thursdays 11-3, and Sundays 1:30-4. Adults $3.00, children $0.50.
This is an elegant example of Victorian Italianate architecture, built in 1853. It is one of those rare restorations that include complete furnishings original to the house.

Macculloch Hall
45 Macculloch Avenue
Open year round, Sundays and Thursdays 1-4. No fee.
Home of George Macculloch, whose creative thinking led to the building of the Morris Canal across the hills of New Jersey in 1831. The house also contains an outstanding collection of Thomas Nast cartoons. Nast lived across the street for many years. A charming 19th century rose garden is in the rear.

Historic Speedwell
Speedwell Avenue and Cory Road, north of town on Route 22. Open May through October, Thursdays and Fridays 12-4, Saturdays and Sundays 1-5. Adults $3, Seniors $2, Children under six are free.
The home of Alfred Vail, where he and Samuel F. B. Morse

perfected and demonstrated the electromagnetic telegraph. This is also where the engine for the first transatlantic steamship, the *Savannah*, was built. Three other eighteenth century houses have also been moved to the property to save them from demolition.

In the late nineteenth century, Morristown was home to about fifty of the presidents of the 100 largest companies in the nation. Many of their mansions still stand and can be seen on walking tours. Most are in private hands and not open to the public.

Jockey Hollow

5 miles south of Morristown on Western Avenue (becomes Jockey Hollow Road) or south on Interstate 287 and follow signs.

"On the 14th [of December 1779, we] reached this wilderness, about 3 miles from Morristown, where we are to build log huts for winter quarters. Our baggage is left in the rear for want of wagons to transport it. The snow on the ground is about two feet deep, and the weather extremely cold." — Dr. James Thacher, Surgeon, Continental Army.

Washington had arrived two weeks earlier, in the middle of a blizzard whipping hail and snow over the New Jersey hills. It would turn out to be the worst winter of the entire century, far worse than that spent at Valley Forge. While Washington and his senior officers were housed in private homes in and around Morristown, the junior officers and troops bedded down in this heavily wooded valley.

They lived in temporary tents or slept on the bare ground under skimpy rags of canvas while they cut trees and built crude log huts. More than 600 acres of prime first growth oaks, maples, chest-

Huts were built without nails and erected as quickly as possible but it was still a couple of months before all the men were sheltered from the bitter winter.

nuts and walnuts were ultimately cut down to provide housing and firewood. Storms came with unremitting frequency, twenty-eight blizzards before the spring finally came. Meanwhile, soldiers would bed down under a worn blanket or rag of canvas and wake up under a foot of snow.

A warmly clothed, well-equipped army would have been able to survive this without a great deal of difficulty, but Washington's army went into it ragged and ill-equipped. Worse, the frequent storms and deep snow made transport of food and supplies — when they could be found — almost impossible.

As the huts slowly rose, snow drifted six feet deep around them. Ten to twelve men huddled together around an open fireplace with green wood burning smokily. Frigid wind blew through the mud-plastered walls. Ultimately, more than 1,000 huts were built, to house some 10,000 officers and enlisted men.

Visitor Center

This is an attractive building, sheltered under huge trees that give the appearance of Jockey Hollow before the troops arrived. It contains a small gift shop and bookstore that must offer every book ever written on any phase of the Revolution in New Jersey. There's a short film that tells the story of that brutal winter. But the highlight of the Center is the reproduction of the interior of one of the huts that were built there. You look down into it from the top of a ramp and wonder how a dozen men could have gotten along with each other in such crowded conditions. Then add, on top of these crowded conditions, the constant smoke from a fire of green wood, the body smells, the extreme cold and the constant hunger. It gives new respect to those who survived it.

Wick House and Farm

When the Pennsylvania Line couldn't put up with it any more and mutinied in January 1781, two of its soldiers spotted twenty-one-year-old Temp (short for Temperance) Wick, daughter of a local farmer, riding her horse home from a visit to her brother-in-law, a local doctor. They grabbed the bridle and told her they needed her horse. She waited until they momentarily let go of the reins, and galloped rapidly off. The soldiers followed, but she beat them to her house, led the horse into her bedroom and shut the door until they left. It's a great story, and you can see the bedroom, but nobody is sure whether the story is true.

The house is a simple farmhouse of the time, simply but comfortably furnished. General St. Clair used it as his headquarters during the bitter winter of '79-'80. In the summer an extensive herb garden is in full bloom, and an apple orchard grows in the distance.

Ringwood

Ringwood Manor

(201) 962-7031

Sloatsburg Road, 2 1/2 miles north of Ringwood. The manor is open May to early October, closed Mondays. On summer weekends and holidays there is a $2.00 per car parking fee. Grounds and gardens open year-round.

One of the reasons Washington chose Morristown as his home base was that out its back door lay the farms and iron mines that would feed and arm his soldiers. Northwestern New Jersey was rife with iron mines, furnaces and forges. Ringwood, in a valley in the Ramapo Mountains, began producing iron in the 1740's. Oddly enough, little iron was produced here during the Revolution because most of the workers went off to fight the war. Many of them were German immigrants and fought on the British side. Other mines and forges in the area filled the gap.

Ringwood Manor, the ironmaster's estate, contains a fine collection of Washington memorabilia, including the map he carried throughout the war.

A major advantage developed out of the worker shortage — it freed up Ringwood's ironmaster, Robert Erskine, to become Washington's Surveyor General. He created highly accurate surveys of most of northern New Jersey, giving Washington much better maps than the British had, thus giving him a distinct advantage in movement. You can lay a tissue tracing of one of his maps over a present-day Rand McNally and find the main roads are drawn almost identically.

Washington visited Ringwood to meet with Erskine at least five times and may have made his headquarters here on occasion. He also re-routed the main highway from Morristown to West Point so that it went past Erskine's manor house.

General Erskine died of pneumonia in 1780 and is buried about 400 yards away from the manor house in a cemetery with about 400 other burials, including many Revolutionary War soldiers.

The original ironmaster's house was torn down or burned down about 1810 and a three-story Federal-style house was built above and behind its site. This has been added to, remodeled, and Victorianized over the years until it reached its present 78-room size, with 24 fireplaces and 250 windows.

Peter Cooper, one of the leading industrialists of the nineteenth century and the founder of Cooper Union in New York, lived here for many years, as did his relative and partner, Abram Hewitt. The house is furnished just as the Cooper and Hewitt families left it. Included is a large collection of Washingtoniana, including Washington's personal pocket map. This large map, measuring about 18" x 36," shows the complete area from above West Point to below Philadelphia. It is stained and spotted from years of being carried around in all kinds of weather and is cracked and torn on the creases where it was folded.

Ringwood Manor is in the middle of Ringwood State Park which includes Skylands, the New Jersey State Botanical Gardens, and Shepherd Lake, a small bathing and boating facility. Behind Ringwood Manor are nice picnicking grounds beside the bouncing Ramapo River.

This is an interesting way of seeing the ruggedly beautiful countryside which contributed so strongly to Washington's efforts.

Also of interest:
Skylands Botanical Gardens
Off Sloatsburg Road about a half mile south of Ringwood Manor, within Ringwood State Park. Follow Morris Road 1 1/2 miles up hill to parking area.

In 1922, Clarence McKenzie Lewis, a wealthy New York investment banker bought a huge estate amassed by another wealthy New Yorker, lawyer Francis Lynde Stetson. He tore down Stetson's magnificent home and built one even more magnificent. He collected and planted trees and plants from all over the world with the help of prestigious landscape designers. After his death the property was taken over briefly by a college and was sold in 1966 to the state of New Jersey, all 1,117 acres.

The state has continued to build on the work that Lewis started. The grounds are gorgeous, the views spectacular. If you are a serious gardener, the plant collection is stupendous. The house is unfurnished and is open only occasionally for special events. It is a restful and relaxing place to calm down from a busy day.

Another Year Wears On

While the men struggled against the elements, Washington struggled against other problems. Inflation had ruined the currency printed by the Continental Congress. It reached the point where it cost more to print the money than the money was worth. Beef and bread, the two main staples for the army, were almost impossible to buy. The beset commander turned to the states for assistance, especially New Jersey and neighboring Pennsylvania, New York, and Delaware. He pleaded for the supplies needed to keep his army alive. The response from New Jersey "saved the army from dissolution," he later said. Spring finally came with the snow gradually disappearing into mud. Supplies began to come in but cash money was still unavailable.

There was good news. Lafayette returned from France with an official promise from the French government of the fleet that Washington had hoped for, but also the promise of an army! Furthermore, the pressure on Washington's northern army had softened. In December, the top British generals had taken 5,000 men and most of the British fleet south. They appeared off South Carolina and laid siege to Charleston.

Martha Washington went back to Mount Vernon, and George moved out of the Ford Mansion. Some of Washington's troops returned to Jockey Hollow the following winter.

In May 1780, two regiments of the 1st Connecticut Brigade shouldered their muskets and began to march home, claiming lack of food, and lack of pay with which to buy any. Their officers finally talked them into unshouldering their muskets and returning to their quarters.

Washington wrote to Congress that "The troops very pointedly mentioned besides their distresses for provisions, their not being paid for five months, and what is of a still more serious and delicate nature in our present circumstances, they mentioned the great depreciation of the money." He also warned Congress that if the Connecticut regiments had walked off that the rest of the army might have followed.

After a town meeting-like debate, the mutineers decided to stay a little while longer.

SEVENTEEN

The Forgotten Battle

In June 1780, there was an unusual battle, in two parts, two weeks apart, that most historians for some reason tend to overlook or to play down as a mere "raid." However, it pitched 6,000 British, Hessians and loyalist volunteers against an unknown number of Continentals and militia. It consisted of two attempts, the first led by the Hessian general Knyphausen, the second by British commander-in-chief Clinton himself, to reach Morristown and capture Washington. It's been called the "forgotten" battle. Others call it the Battle of Springfield.

The winter of 1779-80 was so cold, so bitter cold, the narrow Arthur Kill watercourse between Staten Island and the New Jersey mainland froze so heavily that raids back and forth became simplified, and therefore more frequent. American General William Alexander, often called Lord Stirling, led a mixed group of soldiers across in early January. It was repulsed without much damage done to either side. The British responded several days later with a strong raid on Elizabethtown (now just "Elizabeth") in which they burned down many houses and part of the Presbyterian church.

At British headquarters in New York, a major debate was going on. General Clinton was in the south, in conquered Charleston, with a major part of his army. Hessian General Knyphausen was left in command in New York. He was under heavy pressure from Loyalist leaders, especially New Jersey's last royal governor, William Franklin, to take advantage of Clinton's absence to make a mark of his own. Word of the mutiny of the Connecticut troops was the final straw.

Franklin and his associates knew that while Clinton was out of town Knyphausen would like to make some kind of move that would add luster and glory to his own military record. Nothing he could do while Clinton was present would redound to the German's credit. Now, Franklin pointed out repeatedly, was Knyphausen's chance. *"Grab it! The rebel army is breaking apart. Hit it now! You can end the war right now!"*

As the weather warmed, and there was still no sign of Clinton's return, the Hessian began to accept their plan. He could land an army at Elizabeth Point, push through the little villages of Connecticut Farms (now Union), Springfield, Summit, through Hobart Gap in the Watchungs at the Short Hills, roll up through Chatham, Bottle Hill (now Madison) and have an open road into Morristown. He could capture Washington, the Old Fox, and finish the war while Clinton was still down south. And wouldn't *that* add glory to his name!

At midnight on June 6, 1780, Knyphausen made his move, pushing some 5,000 troops across the narrow Arthur Kill. Under the command of British Brigadier General Thomas Sterling, they mushed through the mud of Elizabeth Point and, as silently as they could, they crept into the night. But a patriot spy had crept through the same mud a few hours earlier and tipped off the local Militia.

A small squad of locals waited by Elizabeth's old Stone Bridge and fired into the darkness at an approaching sound, then raced away into the night. The only casualty of their fire was Brigadier General Thomas Sterling who lay on the ground with a smashed thigh bone.

This tied up the British advance for an hour or so to straighten things out, giving time for a messenger to get to the signal station atop Hobart Gap. In another two hours the word was at Morristown, and Washington began issuing orders. Before daylight, Continental forces were on their way. Just to be sure that this would not be another case of calling out the militia for a false alarm, the instructions to the signal station were to wait until they could see the British soldiers emerging from Elizabethtown before firing off a huge mortar called the Old Sow and lighting the warning fires.

The British finally got reorganized and started out again along what was then Galloping Hill Road and is now Morris Avenue. They passed Liberty Hall, home of New Jersey Governor William Livingston on their left. (The road has since been relocated, and the front door of the house altered to face the new road.) Just past there, shots began to crack out from the woods on either side of the road. The local troop of Continentals under Colonel Elias Dayton was already at work.

One of the beauties of the Watchung Mountains as a shield for Washington at Morristown was that from the long line of peaks one could see forever. From the top of Hobart's Gap, with a good glass, Manhattan was visible. On a hot summer day, moving troops kicked up a high cloud of dust. Through the dust cloud, flashing glints of steel were plainly visible. The Old Sow boomed with a voice heard miles away. A fire crackled quickly into life in a log tower and sent up a cloud of smoke visible for miles. Within a few minutes similar fires were burning north and south along the mountain tops.

Just a month earlier, Governor Livingston had issued orders to all militia colonels north of the Raritan River that in case of alarm, they should muster with their men as quickly as possible at Hobart's Gap. All over the northern part of the state, movement began.

The Reverend James Caldwell, longtime pastor of Elizabethtown's Presbyterian Church, was among those riding furiously along the back roads, acting like a local Paul Revere, waking the locals and mustering the militia. He was a major local figure. Not only did he serve his own church, he rode tirelessly throughout the area, preaching in barns and open fields, helping to found new churches, including the ones in Connecticut Farms and Springfield, and in the town now named after him, Caldwell. Since his own church in Elizabethtown had been burned out in the January raid, he had made Connecticut Farms his headquarters and installed his wife and nine children in a house nearby.

In addition, he had been a loud and provocative preacher of independence both before and after the Declaration. When war came to New Jersey, he joined the Third New Jersey Regiment as chaplain and served in northern New York for a year. Back home, he became deputy quartermaster general of the Continental army, struggling to find supplies and equipment for Washington's army. Local Tories labeled him "The Rebel Parson," and put a price on his head. It was Caldwell who had set up the series of alarm fires and cannon along the heights. Now he was rousing his countrymen to stop the invading army that was slowly approaching his family.

It took about three hours for the invaders to creep the three miles uphill from Liberty Hall to Connecticut Farms as, remembering Concord and Lexington, they paused at each stone wall or copse of trees to clear out the militia before advancing. That was just the beginning. It became an all-day battle just to advance through Connecticut Farms to the larger village of Springfield. By dusk, the British army, despite their huge advantage in manpower, had been fought to a standstill before it was able to reach Hobart Gap. Interestingly, it had been brought to a halt mainly by the local troops, militia and a few New Jersey Continentals. Washington's troops didn't arrive until late in the afternoon.

The British retreated back to a small rise northwest of Connecticut Farms and dug in for the night. From there they would retreat back to Staten Island.

However, during the fighting the British had begun burning and looting. In one house, three ladies were huddled, expecting that, as was customary, the soldiers would leave them alone. One was suckling an eight-month-old baby. One soldier peered into the window raised his musket and fired. The nursing mother died instantly. She was Hannah Caldwell, the parson's wife. His other children had been removed to Chatham, but it was felt that the rigors of the trip might dry up Hannah's milk, so she had stayed.

When the soldiers set that house on fire, her friends dragged her body outside. The soldiers went on to fire her husband's church as well. Both buildings would be rebuilt as soon as the war was over and are open to the public now.

When the British retreated to Staten Island, they learned that General Clinton was due to return from the Carolinas within a few days. Sudden shock! *What would Clinton think of the Loyalists handling of Knyphausen? What would he think of Knyphausen going off on his own? and for not being successful in his efforts?*

Clinton was at first angry, then decided it wasn't a bad idea. Under *his* leadership, and with additional troops, it could put an end to the war. Two weeks after their first try, they set off again across the narrow Arthur Kill.

This expedition was a repeat of the first. The Old Sow boomed again, and the alarm fires smoked up the skies. The local militia slowed the approach and the serious fighting began when the two-pronged advance of the invaders reached the burnt-out Connecticut Farms. Here they ran into organized resistance from Washington's own personal guard and from Continentals with a bit of light artillery. The fighting became fierce at the little Rahway River. Finally, the British forced their way across and into the area now known as Millburn. But the battle had been harsh, the day was hot, and the British could see reinforcements coming down the hill from Morristown. They turned and headed back to Staten Island. The locals harried them all the way. This was the last major battle in the north.

Union
Liberty Hall
1003 Morris Avenue (908) 527-0400
Open Wednesdays through Sundays, April through December, other times by appointment. Fee: $10.00 adults, $8.00 senior citizens, children ages 6-17 $4.00. Under 6, free.

In 1772, William Livingston was a well-to-do New York lawyer and member of the politically-active Livingston clan. At that time, he built a fine large home in New Jersey as a vacation retreat. Within three years New York had become so dangerously revolutionary that he moved his family across the river permanently. Two hundred twenty years later, in 1995, the last direct descendant of the family living in the house, Mary Alice Barney Kean, passed away at age 92. She was an ardent supporter of historic preservation and, for years before her death, spent her time preparing the house to become a museum. In May 2000, Governor Christie Whitman officially opened the house to the public as the Liberty Hall Museum. Among the guests was former New Jersey Governor Thomas Kean, another scion of the family.

In the gift shop his and-hers T-shirts are for sale. The first reads, "George Washington never slept here...." The second one says, "...but Martha did." And the bed she slept in is still in a second floor front bedroom, still in family use until just a few years ago. Across the hall is the back bedroom where then-President Gerald Ford slept.

In the dining room, they point out the window that an early step-daughter eloped through, choosing that window so she could step onto the beehive oven under it. Her fellow-eloper, William Henry Harrison, later became President. That's the kind of house it is.

As soon as New Jersey became a state in 1776, Livingston was elected its first governor. Because the house was dangerously close to Elizabethtown, Livingston moved inland, living for a time in Basking Ridge and later in Parsippany. He and Washington worked closely together throughout the War and became good friends.

At the time of the June 1780 invasion, two of Livingston's three daughters (all highly attractive and known to New Jersey society as "The Three Graces") were living there. They flirted with the young British officers and talked them into leaving a guard over the house so that it wouldn't be looted or damaged.

Since then, seven generations of Livingstons and Keans have lived there — and apparently never thrown anything away. Almost all of the furniture and decorations are family pieces, including one whole room full of children's toys. It's a fascinating and highly historic house, all fifty-one rooms of it.

Caldwell's Home and Church
Home: 909 Caldwell Avenue (908) 964-9047
Open by appointment only.
Church: Stuyvesant Avenue near Chestnut Street (908) 688-3164
Open during normal church hours.

Both the Reverend James Caldwell's home and his church were burned by the British in the first phase of the 1780 battle. His wife was killed during the battle, and he was murdered a year and a half later. The present house, called "Caldwell's Home," and the Connecticut Farms Presbyterian Church were built in 1782 on the old foundations. Both are open to the public.

The Union Township Historical Society operates a small exhibit of early life in the house. There is also an exhibit detailing the life of one of New Jersey's most colorful characters, General William "Scotch Willie" Maxwell. He earned the nickname not only because he was originally from Scotland, but also because he loved that land's native fermentation He led troops in many major actions of the Revolution, including the battles of Connecticut Farms and Springfield.

Springfield
Springfield Presbyterian Church
Morris Avenue and Church Mall

Now in the main business district of bustling Springfield, the Presbyterian Church was the last stand of the American forces during the Battle of Springfield on June 23, 1780.

One of the famous tales of the battle has it that when the American artillery was running short of paper wadding to hold the powder and balls in their cannons, they put up a loud cry. Pastor Caldwell heard their appeal and dashed to the church, broke in and grabbed up armloads of Watts hymnals. Tossing them to the men, he shouted "Give 'em Watts boys...give 'em Watts! The men grabbed the books, tore them up, stuffed the pages into the mouths of their cannons and continued firing, helping to halt the British. Before retreating, the British set fire to the church. The present building was built in 1791 to replace it.

Cannonball House
126 Morris Avenue (973) 376-4784
Only open by appointment.

This house, owned by the Hutchins family during the revolution, was one of only four homes left standing after the Battle of Springfield, June 23, 1780. It was not burned by the retreating British because, a) it was used as a hospital for wounded British soldiers, or b) it was owned by an acknowledged Tory, or c) it was a popular bar. Or maybe all three. Take your choice.

It was located at about the high-water mark for the British before they rested for lunch and decided to go home. Other than the fact that it was a survivor, its main claim to fame hangs on its outer wall — a lump of lead a little smaller than a baseball. No one knows whether it was fired by the Americans or the British. It's probably a three-pounder. It stuck in the wall of the building during the battle.

The house is owned and operated by the Springfield Historical Society. A very pretty herb garden is in back of the house.

Elizabeth
Boxwood Hall
1073 East Jersey Street
Open Wednesday - Saturday 10-12, 1-6, Sunday 1-6. Free.

Elias Boudinot was one of New Jersey's strongest leaders before and during the Revolution. He was a delegate to the Continental Congress, was elected as its president in 1783, and was the official signer of the Treaty of Peace with Great Britain. He was a strong supporter and good friend of Washington's.

He built this house in the 1750's. Originally, it had wings on either side. These were taken down in the 1800's when many parts of the house were altered.

Elizabeth (then called "Elizabethtown") was just across the narrow, 100-yard wide Arthur Kill from Staten Island, where for most of the war some 35,000 or more British, Hessian and colonial troops were barracked. Also now living on Staten Island were many civilian Tory or loyalist sympathizers who no longer dared to live in their New Jersey homes. This left Elizabethtown wide open to raids, both official and spur-of-the-moment. In turn, many of the local patriots took their turns at raiding the Staten Island shores. Elizabethtown was the launching point for the Hessian invasion of June 1780 called the Battle of Springfield.

As Washington neared the end of his long trek up from Mount Vernon to assume the presidency in 1789, he stopped in at Boxwood Hall to see his old friend Boudinot. His party was entertained here at a gala lunch.

Years later when Lafayette returned to the United States in 1825 on the occasion of the fiftieth anniversary of the Revolution, he also stopped in here to see Boudinot and be entertained.

The original property of the house extended to the Elizabeth River, about 200 yards to the south. The path up from the river to the front door was bordered on both sides by boxwood shrubs, hence the name "Boxwood Hall." Many boxwoods still fringe the front of the house.

First Presbyterian Church
42 Broad Street (908) 353-1518

This was Reverend James Caldwell's main church. It was burned during a Tory raid in the cold winter of January 1780 and rebuilt. The steeple is original. Armed sentries used to perch on the steeple to watch for unfriendly Tory raiders. Caldwell would carry pistols to the pulpit while he preached. It includes a museum. The cemetery is also of interest.

The First Presbyterian Church in Elizabeth was a patriot center during the war, and its parson, Reverend James Caldwell was a local firebrand and hero. His wife, Hannah, was killed during the Battle of Springfield. Parson Caldwell was murdered in November 1781, while going about his work in Elizabethtown. His killer was hung nearby.

Also of interest:
Nathaniel Bunnell Homestead
1045 East Jersey Street

After many years of slow decline, Elizabeth is pulling itself up by its bootstraps with the Elizabeth Urban Enterprise Zone. Its headquarters are just a few doors away from Boxwood Hall in the Nathaniel Bunnell Homestead.

Nathaniel Bunnell was one of a company of 80 men, called the "Associators," who founded Elizabethtown in 1664. He built his house sometime between 1664 and 1682. It's the oldest surviving house in Elizabeth. Currently in use as headquarters for the Elizabeth Urban Enterprise Zone, it is therefore not open to the general public. However, you can walk around it and see the early forms of construction from the outside. While there is no known direct connection to Washington, he would have seen it when visiting either Boxwood Hall or the Belcher-Ogden House across the street.

Belcher-Ogden Mansion
1046 East Jersey Street (908) 351-2500

Directly across the street from the Bunnell Homestead, this early colonial house, built in the late 1750's, was the residence of Jonathan Belcher, New Jersey's royal governor from 1751 to 1757, and of the Ogden family, longtime local and statewide leaders. After Belcher died in 1757, William Peartree Smith bought the house. His daughter married Elisha Boudinot, Elias' brother. Washington, Lafayette, and Alexander Hamilton all attended the wedding.

On February 10, 1780, as part of a large raid on Elizabethtown, the house was ransacked by British soldiers hunting for Smith's son-in-law.

In 1797, the old mansion was bought by Colonel Aaron Ogden, a member of an early Elizabethtown family. Ogden was a local hero throughout the Revolution. In 1775, he helped capture a British supply ship that enabled Washington to continue his siege of Boston. At Monmouth, his reconnaissance gave Washington the information he needed for victory. And at Yorktown, he led a storming party that was one of the keys to Cornwallis's surrender. Washington gave him a special commendation for this effort. Later, he became the second Governor of New Jersey to live in this house.

Apparently, the original home on this site was a one-room building of British-made bricks, probably in the 1670's. This room is now the first room on the left as you enter the home.

Nearly two dozen other Revolutionary War era homes are in this same area, especially in the 1000 and 1100 blocks of East Jersey Street. None of these are open to the public but are worth a stroll past. East Jersey Street extends east to the Arthur Kill. Just to the left is a large public deck overlooking the water. You can see the closeness of Staten Island and the narrowness of the waterway. Look over there and imagine 35,000 of the enemy glaring back at you.

Towaco
The Henry Doremus House

490 Main Road. Not open to the public at this time. Funds are being raised for restoration.

Between the two halves of the Battle of Springfield, Washington brought part of his army north to shepherd a wagon train of supplies, badly needed at West Point. It was also a precautionary move in case the British invasion of New Jersey was just a feint to hide a major attack up the Hudson River.

His troops had reached Rockaway Bridge, about fifteen miles from Springfield, and Washington had commandeered the Doremus House where he spent the night in the right hand room. Next morning news reached him that the British were making another attempt at breaking through to Morristown. He immediately turned and headed back.

Wherever Washington stayed was a "headquarters." He had an eye for his creature comforts, having spent far too many nights on the ground under the stars. He usually tried to lodge in the best house in whatever area he happened to be. In this case you can imagine what the rest of the homes in the area looked like.

Washington usually chose the best house in the neighborhood for his headquarters. This little two-room stone house was the best he could find in what is now Towaco.

This is typical mid-1700's Jersey Dutch stone construction. One room would have been used as an all purpose kitchen-dining-living room, the other would have been a sleeping room for the parents. Each room had its own outside door. Children slept in the loft covering both rooms. There was a root cellar under each room.

A year later, French troops on their way to Yorktown camped in the surrounding fields and orchards. The Doremus House still has its original fireplace and its original wide-plank flooring.

Wayne
Dey Mansion
99 Totowa Road
(973) 696-1776
Open Wednesday - Friday 1-4:30, Saturday - Sunday 10-12, 1-4:30. Closed on major holidays. Group tours by appointment. Adults: $1.00, children under 10 are free. Take Route 80 to Exit 55, to Union Boulevard. At the second light make a left onto Crews Street. After the stop sign continue straight onto Totowa Road. The museum is about a mile on the right.

The Deys were early Jersey Dutch settlers, arriving here in the 1600's. Derick Dey built this fine manor house in the 1740's, apparently with an infusion of English ideas in the Georgian design. Derick's son, Theunis, was an active patriot during the Revolution, and a colonel in the local county militia. This brought him into frequent contact with George Washington. When Washington moved the main body of his troops to the

Dey Mansion looks completely Georgian English design from the front but completely Jersey Dutch from the side.

nearby Preakness Valley (now mainly Wayne) after the first battle of Springfield, Dey (pronounced Dye) invited him to use his home as headquarters. Washington occupied the house off and on for three months in 1780. One legend has it that Washington moved here because of intelligence that he was about to be kidnapped in Morristown.

The main impetus of the war had moved south and General Nathaniel Greene had been sent to command the southern forces. Washington positioned his remaining forces to watch the British in New York, and stay where he could move quickly to protect either Philadelphia or the Hudson River. The battle to find food and pay for his troops continued. While staying here, Washington received word that French General Rochambeau wanted to meet with him in Rhode Island. Returning from this trip, he looked forward to a visit with his faithful general, Benedict Arnold and his lovely wife, Peggy. But Arnold wasn't there, and Peggy Shippen Arnold was still in bed. It seemed Arnold must be across the river at West Point. Washington was rowed across the river. Arnold hadn't been seen there all day. The general returned to Arnold's house just as a soldier rode up with a sheaf of papers taken from a "John Anderson" — obviously a British spy. "Anderson" turned out to be Major John Andre, General Clinton's highest ranking intelligence officer. Arnold had learned of his capture just before Washington's arrival and realizing that his treason was exposed, he had escaped downriver to the ship that had brought Andre to the scene.

Andre was taken to the village of Tappan, New York, and imprisoned in Mabie's Tavern. After Andre was tried and hung, Washington returned to Dey Mansion. During the trial, Washington lived in the nearby DeWint House (which see, page 107).

The Dey house is an interesting combination of English and Dutch architecture. It has the graceful Dutch gambrel roof over the four-square Georgian arrangement of windows in a brick front. The huge oak timbers and handsomely-cut brown stones are Dutch, the plastered walls inside are English. The separate-but-attached kitchen wing is Dutch, designed to keep the heat of the fireplace out of the main house during the summer months, and the danger of fire out year-round.

The furnishings range from the 1600's to the late 1700's, but few are connected directly to Washington. The mansion is the meeting place of several Revolutionary War organizations including Robert Erskine's Militia, a reenactment group that recreates military life during the Revolution. It stages several events a year.

The house is on a two-acre property that includes several replica outbuildings, a traditional knot garden for medicinal and cooking herbs, and a picnic grounds. The property is owned and managed by the Passaic County Department of Parks and Recreation.

Little organized military activity occurred in the north during Washington's stay here.

Nearby:
While in Wayne visit the Schuyler-Colfax House. See page 63.

E I G H T E E N

The Problems Continue as the Long Struggle Comes to a Peak

The year 1780 closed with most of the major action in the south and with Washington keeping the rest of the British army cooped up on Manhattan and Staten Islands. His financial and supply problems continued as severely as before despite the influx of arms and money from France. The new year brought new problems.

On January 1, 1781 the Pennsylvania Line, 2,000 of Washington's most reliable veteran troops, rose up in disgust at the poor food and lack of pay. Led by their sergeants, they shouldered their arms, marched out of Jockey Hollow and headed south toward Trenton, where they could cross the Delaware back to their home state. They paused at Princeton to have discussions with their commander, General "Mad Anthony" Wayne. They took over Nassau Hall while the palaver dragged on.

Washington himself was with other troops in Newburgh, New York. He was afraid that if he left them to come to Princeton, these troops would also mutiny. Eventually, the state of Pennsylvania found sufficient cash money to satisfy the mutineers' demands, and most of them marched back to Jockey Hollow.

Several other smaller mutinies cropped up but were put down, one with the ringleaders being shot by a firing squad of their own cohorts to make an example for others who might have mutiny in mind.

In the summer of 1781, in a rapid but secret movement, Washington sent all his troops hurrying south to Virginia where General Greene had managed to maneuver British General Cornwallis into a trap in the little village of Yorktown. To prepare for this movement Washington built up a big charade to keep the rest of the British army in New York. He built big ovens, big enough to bake 400 loaves of bread at a time in Chatham, a village on the direct route from Morristown to Staten Island.

He "accidentally" dropped messages about a forthcoming attack on Staten Island. The French army was marching west from Rhode Island and Washington made a lot of noise about their joining him for an attack on Manhattan. The French did join him, but then both armies rushed to Virginia to meet Cornwallis in the last major battle of the war.

The main road to Yorktown led right in front of Mount Vernon, so Washington was able to visit his home for the first time in more than six years. Most of that time had been spent in New Jersey.

Chatham

The eastern end of Chatham's main street — Route 124 — has many antique homes, several of them date back to the Revolution. Chatham, on the Passaic River, was on the direct route to Morristown. It was a strongly pro-Revolution town from early on, being named after William Pitt, Earl of Chatham, who was one of America's strongest supporters in England's Parliament.

Two houses are of particular interest:

The Jacob Morrell House
63 Main Street
Washington headquartered here for several days and wrote some seventeen letters headed "Chatham" while here. This was in 1781 when he was trying his best to trick the British into thinking he and the French army were going to invade New York. The house is open to the public, but as a fine and expensive restaurant named Scalini Fedeli.

The corner to the east was the location of a building where Shepard Kollock published the *New-Jersey Journal*, New Jersey's first newspaper. At the time of the Battle of Springfield, Kollock felt sufficiently afraid to pack up his press and his type and hide them until the battle was over.

The William Day House
70 Main Street
Across from the Morrell House, this house is recognizable by its prominent Dutch oven. The house was built in 1780 when the owner was a captain in the Morris County militia. It is a wallpaper store now.

Wrapping It Up

The next two buildings are no longer in New Jersey but were important to two different important events of the Revolution, Arnold's treachery and the end of the war. However, they may have been in New Jersey at one time. It was just two years before the war started, in 1773, when the exact border between New York and New Jersey was finally determined. This decision placed these two buildings a few hundred yards into New York state.

Tappan, New York
The Old '76 House

Main Street just south of Old Tappan Road. Take Palisades Interstate Parkway north from Fort Lee to Exit 5. South on Route 303 to first right, King's Highway. This leads into Tappan. Old '76 House is on right just past stoplight.

This typical Jersey Dutch red sandstone house with its gambrel roof and big porch was bought by Casparus Mabie in 1753 and converted into a tavern. It became a meeting place for local patriots. The "Orangetown Resolutions," signed here on July 4, 1774, called for separation from England exactly two years before the Declaration of Independence.

British Major John Andre was held prisoner in the Mabie Tavern while being tried as a spy across the road in the Dutch Reformed Church. (The present church on the site, the third, was built in 1835.) The tavern has been "restored" several times with most restorations retaining an "Andre's Cell" room. The Old '76 House is still a restaurant. The food is (at this writing) both good and reasonably priced.

Of additional interest:

Go out of the '76 House door, turn left at the corner of Old Tappan Road and go uphill a little less than a half a mile to a marker, then left up Andre Hill to a monument marking the spot where

Major Andre was hung and buried. In 1821, his remains were taken home to England and placed in Westminster Abbey.

De Wint House

20 Livingston Street (914) 359-1359
Take Palisades Interstate Parkway north from Fort Lee to Exit 5.
Go south on Route 303 to first right (King's Highway). Follow to
center of Tappan. Go through traffic light and bear left. Follow
signs.

Daniel De Clark was a well-to-do Dutch merchant and brewer when he built this house in the wilderness in 1700. He built not of local stone or logs but of imported Dutch brick and proudly spelt out "1700" in two-foot high letters of a different colored brick in the front wall. He also surrounded his open fireplace with 70 purple Delft tiles of biblical scenes. DeClark served locally as a magistrate and as a local militia captain. No one now knows when he sold his house or when he passed on, but in 1746 the house came into the ownership of Johannis and Antje De Wint of New York City. He was a wealthy plantation owner from the West Indies. His descendants lived here until 1818. Living with them in August 1780 were their daughter and son-in-law Frederickus Blauvelt. He was a major in the local militia. Washington used this house on four different occasions.

When General Washington showed up in the area to spend a couple of weeks examining its defenses, Major Blauvelt offered him lodging and the general accepted. Then he went on his way up to meet French General Rochambeau in Hartford, Connecticut.

Washington returned to the DeWint house and stayed there while British Major Andre was tried in the local church, was convicted and hung on a nearby hilltop. Washington refused to attend the trial and is said to have closed the blinds of the house so that he couldn't see when Andre was led away to be hung. The table at which he signed the execution order is still in the DeWint house.

Just a year later, with the victory at Yorktown, Virginia, the shooting war was over, but the peace still had to be established. The British still maintained a strong force in New York City, and Washington established his major base at Newburgh, New York. General Clinton had been called back to England, and General Sir Guy Carleton had come down from Canada to take his place. On May 5, 1782, the two commanders met at Tappan.

Carleton came up river with his suite of officers on a British warship. Washington came down from Newburgh and met him at the landing. They went up to the DeWint house and enjoyed a sumptuous dinner catered by none other than "Black Sam" Fraunce, the noted New York City tavern keeper. Next day, Washington visited Sir Guy on board the warship. The occasion was particularly noteworthy in that for the first time in history, a British king's warship fired a salute to the American flag. The next day the two commanders agreed on the final terms and arrangements for the evacuation of New York.

However, a provisional peace treaty wasn't signed until November 1782, and didn't become effective until January 20,1783. On April 19, 1783, exactly eight years to the day after the first musket fire at Lexington Green, Washington officially proclaimed a cessation of hostilities. The treaty was finally signed in Paris on September 3, 1783. The British had agreed to evacuate New York City on November 1 but had a difficult time finding sufficient transport to carry not only their troops but also the thousand-odd Loyalist Tories who demanded to be taken along. At long last, on November 25, 1783, the last British troops left American soil.

Just before the British evacuation, Washington was traveling from Hackensack to West Point on November 11 when a major snowstorm struck. The always hospitable DeWints and Blauvelts took them in. Mrs. John DeWint described it in a letter:

Dear Maria:

I was very happy to receive a letter from you and find you were Comfortably Settled in your winter quarters before the great Snow Storm which nobody remembers the like but myself,... as it was the first snow I ever saw, and was the cause of my enjoying the Company of General Washington for nearly three days. ... He was going to West point with eight or ten officers to march the troops to the City to take Possession when the British Evacuated it, they all called to visit your Grandfathers and were detained by the Snow Storm. I introduced Cards by way of amusement. Colonel Humphries told me it was the first time the General had played cards since the Commencement of the Revolution.

As a young man, barely twenty-one, Washington had joined the local Masonic Lodge at Alexandria, Virginia. He remained an active Mason all his life. In 1932, the 200th anniversary of Washington's birth, the Grand Lodge of Masons of the State of New York bought the old house to save it from destruction. It presently maintains the DeWint house and a small Masonic museum in an adjoining building.

The house itself is small. One wonders how the DeWints, the Blauvelts and Washington with "8 or ten officers" could squeeze into it to wait out a three-day snow storm. A nineteenth-century drawing shows an addition to the house that has long since disappeared. Perhaps it was there when Washington was.

"Crossroads" and "Cockpit" of the Revolution

New Jersey has been called both the cockpit of the Revolution and the crossroads of the Revolution. As this is being written (Winter 2003), there is a bill before Congress to establish in New Jersey a "Crossroads of the American Revolution National Heritage Area," under the aegis of the National Park Service. The 'Area' would cover a large portion of the state from Gloucester County in the south to Bergen County in the north. It would include most of the scores of battlefields and other significant sites that had New Jersey at the center of the war from start to finish.

If passed, the designation will focus public attention on the 'Area's' historic significance, will make technical assistance available and bring Federal funding — up to $1 million — for preserving and improving important sites. It will tie together the publicly and privately-owned historic sites in guides and interpretive signing.

The bill was introduced in the Senate by Senator Jon Corzine, and in the House by Representative Rodney Frelinghuysen, a direct descendant of one of New Jersey's founding families (see "The Old Dutch Parsonage," page 79).

There are countless sites in New Jersey that relate to the War of the Revolution, many of them beyond the scope of the proposed Heritage Area. They include almost every part of the state that was settled by the 1770's. From furthest northwest to lowest southeast, New Jersey was undoubtedly the most fought-over state of the original thirteen.

In Montague, on the Delaware River and touching New York State, Iroquois Indians came down from the Mohawk Valley to raid in July 1779. This was also on the safest route from the capital in Philadelphia to the New England states, and was used by all of the well-known delegates, such as John Adams, John Hancock, and others.

At the opposite end of the state, Cape May, there are on display the remaining ribs of a British cruiser forced ashore in August

1778. All along the New Jersey shores, both east and west, are the scenes of raids, skirmishes and naval actions. In fact, one of the last actions of the war was a loyalist raid on Tom's River on August 23, 1782, almost a year after the deciding battle at Yorktown.

Bergen County, the most northeastern county in the state, and just across the Hudson River from British-held Manhattan, suffered more than 100 raids. New Bridge, the location of Steuben House (see page 23) was raided seven times. When the wood shingles on the roof of Steuben House were replaced a few years ago, they were found to be riddled with musket balls.

Elizabeth, just across the narrow Arthur Kill from British and Hessian troops on Staten Island, was raided forty-two times. The south end of the Arthur Kill empties into Raritan Bay behind Sandy Hook. There were eleven different naval actions in those waters.

In the western part of the state, in aptly named National Park, New Jersey, is Red Bank Battlefield Park, site of Fort Mercer. This fort, along with Fort Mifflin, on the Pennsylvania side of the river, was built to protect the Delaware River approaches to Philadelphia. British General Howe avoided them by approaching Philadelphia through Chesapeake Bay, but eventually had to destroy both forts so that his supply ships could reach the city. This took nearly two months, with Mercer holding out three weeks longer than Mifflin. The park, which includes the original farmhouse on the site, is open year-round.

Salem, New Jersey's most westerly point, was the target of British foragers, 1,500 strong, in 1778 while the British occupied Philadelphia. They surprised and destroyed bodies of local militia at nearby Hancock's and Quinton Bridges.

Deep in the wilderness of the Pine Barrens is the restored village of Batsto, a key provider of iron to help fight the war. This iron was not dug from the ground but rather from the numerous streams flowing slowly through the Barrens. Iron particles in the water settled in niches and corners and accumulated where it could be mined. In the northwest is Oxford Furnace which processed iron found in the more usual fashion, and Shippen Manor the big home of its ironmaster.

There are, literally, scores of other historic sites like these throughout the state. They are not included in this book because

Washington had little or nothing to do with them. Also, many of them are privately owned and occupied such as the home of John Honeyman, Washington's spy, and are not open to the public. Their owners don't especially like total strangers peering through their windows.

Almost every early municipality has some kind of marker. Montclair has a brass plaque on a boulder marking where Washington stopped while en route from Preakness to Springfield. Nearby Orange has a Dispatch Rider statue in front of the local Presbyterian church where many Revolutionary War soldiers are buried. In River Vale, a small park marks the burial site of patriot cavalry killed in an episode called Baylor's Massacre. Chestnut Neck, along the unspoiled Mullica River, was a haven for privateers who raided British shipping. The British mounted a major effort to attack this "nest of pirates" and wiped out the village and the fort protecting it. A monument commemorates the event. In Lincoln Park an old sandstone house, now a dentist's office, was a tavern on a frequently used road to West Point and the north. Washington undoubtedly stopped there, but there's no proof of it.

New Jersey has obviously changed considerably since it was just a land route between two major cities, noted mainly for the richness of its farmland. It has become one of the most populous states despite also being one of the smallest. It is the most densely populated state of the union. Despite this population pressure, the state has done amazingly well at preserving its historic treasures. It is well worth exploring. Have fun, be inspired, but take only photos, leave only footprints.

Index

F